LEAVING MY MEGACHURCH LIFE

A HOLY UNEXPECTED EXIT

Copyright © Renee Smith 2020

ISBN 978-1-7343422-0-8
ISBN 978-1-7343422-1-5

All rights reserved. No part of this book may be reproduced or transmitted in any form or by any means, electronic or mechanical, including photocopying, recording, scanning or any information storage and retrieval system without prior permission of the publisher, except as provided by United States of America copyright law.

Scripture taken from the New King James Version®. Copyright © 1982 by Thomas Nelson. Used by permission. All rights reserved.

Cover photo: Rodion Kutsaev, Unsplash
Cover Design & Interior Layout: Frank Shaw, 99designs
Editor: Doreen Arnott

ACKNOWLEDGEMENTS

This book was self-published. The amount invested in this book prior to its publication was a few thousand dollars (this included costs for editing, cover design, interior layout and the purchase of ISBN numbers). About a third of the total cost was covered by a modest but successful *Kickstarter* campaign.

I would like to thank each backer for their support in bringing this project to fruition, including a special thanks to the individuals who elected to fund my project from different places in the world without having met me. I am especially grateful for the support of **Dave and Laura Green** as well as **Bob and Beth Messacar.** They contributed to this publication and personal endeavor in a significant way, even though they had not read the manuscript.

Finally, I would like to thank my **parents** for their love and support, and I would like to express gratitude for my husband, **Steven,** for his insight and encouragement.

...but exhort one another daily, while it is called "Today," lest any of you be hardened through the deceitfulness of sin.

Hebrews 3:13 (NKJV)

CONTENTS

Acknowledgements...i
Preface..vi
A Note from the Author...viii

Part I

Chapter 1:   Unexpected...1
Chapter 2:   Knocked Down, Not Out...11
Chapter 3:   The Golden Ticket...18
Chapter 4:   A Tilted Head...21
Chapter 5:   A Costly Decision...28
Chapter 6:   Move In, or Move Out..33
Chapter 7:   Leaving...42
Chapter 8:   Pride...47

Part II

Chapter 9:   Good Deeds..57
Chapter 10: Vision & Validation...65
Chapter 11: Small Groups..73
Chapter 12: Relationships...79
Chapter 13: Church ≠ God..87
Chapter 14: Giving..94
Chapter 15: Church...102
Chapter 16: Scope..109
Chapter 17: Pastors..114
Chapter 18: Authority..122

Epilogue...129
Final Thoughts from the Author...132

PREFACE

This book was not the result of some knee-jerk reaction, and it was not hastily or emotionally written. I did not elect to leave a beloved church with an aspiration to recount details concerning that decision, especially for others to hear or read about. I also never expected to come face-to-face with several personal sins or feel an overwhelming notion to share about them. Generally, I am a private person. However, I don't know quite how to put this, but choosing to write this book did not feel much like a choice.

One night, about a year following my resignation from the megachurch, I felt utterly compelled to write–so I did. I wrote furiously for hours, unaware of anything transpiring with my typing apart from an outpouring of several subconscious thoughts. They surfaced altogether and revolved around a church experience that, in my estimation, had gone sorrowfully wrong.

Closing my laptop a little before dawn, I retreated to my room and fell into bed with my mind and fingers at rest. Before drifting to sleep, I wondered, *Did something just happen, other than a personal journaling session?* Whatever had taken place was certainly unusual. In trying to fall asleep several hours earlier, I did not plan to embrace insomnia and an all-encompassing writing session. Moreover, I had never considered recording my experience for others to read. Regardless, the notion to bring this piece to its final form was unrelenting. Feeling overcome by a determination and personal resolve that I had never experienced, this book was ultimately born.

Shortly before this work was put into print, I took a break from a final editing pass. Sitting with a mug of hot tea, I reached for a book that I had just brought home from the library. Cracking it open, the book's Preface immediately read as if large chunks of my heart had spilled onto its page:

My soul is at rest. I have done to the best of my understanding what God seemed to require of me with a relentless passion... Sometimes God assigns us a message that is more radical than we'd choose...and requires more transparency than we'd...invite. I am being as honest as I know how to be when I say that I did not write these pages by simple preference...What God does with what He's required is His business.

Beth Moore
Preface, "When Godly People Do Ungodly Things"

A NOTE FROM THE AUTHOR

First, the names and places in these pages have been changed. This includes the names of various Christian organizations, their locations, and those of most individuals. With his blessing, I have chosen only to include the identity of my husband, Steven.

Please note that in electing to change the name of the megachurch, I did not do so because the pages ahead are somehow slandering toward it; in fact, I would be grieved if they were. Additionally, I have not chosen to disguise the megachurch's name believing readers will somehow be unable to determine its true identity. I have chosen to conceal the real congregation because knowing its name is of little consequence compared to observing its mode of operation, something that may prove helpful to others by serving as an example.

In news stories or those told around the dinner table, I believe the actions we hear about are often overshadowed by the identity of the people reported to be doing those actions. In approaching the story within this book, I would like the audience to focus on the types of activities happening within the megachurch and not on the identity of the church itself. I hope that each reader who approaches the narrative in this manner will be better equipped to live as an astute congregant and may elect to make a personal decision: to own greater responsibility in recognizing potential pitfalls within their respective congregation.

On the other hand, each reader who ultimately focuses on the church's true name will likely miss this book's message. Such a reader may be found gawking at other people rather than humbly learning from their actions, specifically those behaviors the reader calls into question. After all, no individual is above sin, regardless of the form it takes.

Second, an integral experience for every reader is the unique ability to be wrapped into a story. In turn, I believe a writer maintains the responsibility to include enough information for readers to take part in this journey.

The following pages in-part describe a financial decision

facing one megachurch in the Bible Belt. In the first iterations of the manuscript, real dollar values were not included because financial figures seemed to be secondary information to the greater, overarching story. However, later in the editing process, I decided to include real dollars because I was convinced that they were an important part of my narrative and integral for the person electing to read it.

I believe the inclusion of financial details will enable each reader to have an autonomous and unique reaction to the situation described, just as I experienced when faced with the unfolding circumstances in real-time. Readers will be able to form their own opinions, as perceptions vary from person-to-person when considering money in terms of a thousand dollars, one hundred thousand dollars or a million dollars.

In sharing specific monetary information concerning the church, I do not believe I am exposing information that is private. At the time of these events, the megachurch shared the same financial numbers during one weekend's services, worship gatherings that anyone in the public had been welcome to attend.

Finally, this book has been divided into two distinct sections. Though uniquely different, the two parts have been composed to portray a unified message. Neither half is intended to be foremost biographical in nature, either about the megachurch or the author. I wrote these pages to remind Christian readers not to quiet their consciences or grow numb to observations that may be indicative of sin that is lurking—in them or their church life. After all, the primary objective of church participation is not personal fulfillment but a life that honors Christ and embodies what he taught: to recognize sin and turn from it.

Part I

SURPRISED, TWICE OVER

(coming and going from the megachurch)

Chapter 1

UNEXPECTED

*A man's heart plans his way,
But the LORD directs his steps.*

Proverbs 16:9 (NKJV)

No one is exempt from uncertainty; I just tend to pretend I am.

My father became unexpectedly wheelchair dependent several years ago. Adjusting in the aftermath was challenging, but my family and I came to a place of acceptance. Not long ago, Dad's struggle to move safely from the bed to his wheelchair became a new reality, one much harder to reconcile. The complications from medical care gone wrong in addition to a relatively recent Parkinson's diagnosis have affected my life deeply, despite facing my father's obstacles in-person only a handful of times each year.

When I visit my dad, sometimes I find that energy and optimism are long gone before the given day ends and the next one dawns. Meanwhile, I want to be of good help to him, but I observe a deficit in my ability as I simultaneously struggle to be positive and patient in my efforts. I feel grief over his situation, recognizing that the struggle of his daily life will never change for the better. Moreover, I mourn the fact that his personal hardship is now my family's trial because of the assistance and care he increasingly requires.

I know most people encounter challenges like this at some point in life, but I still find myself wholly surprised at the unfolding of them. Unpleasant feelings surface as a result, emotions I am not sure how to navigate. Denial creeps in, a bizarre phenomenon that compels me to reach out to my therapist friend because my brain cannot accept certain truths that are plain to the eye.

Loss happens. Injury deems the finish line an impossibility. A spouse leaves, or one never enters the picture in the first place. A disease descends or is diagnosed in someone we love. While God doesn't waste experiences, I find it hard to wait for understanding or a sense of purpose concerning them. Then again, I realize such holy discernment is not something God promises.

While Dad navigates his new normal and Mom wears thin as his primary caregiver, I reside a few states away and grieve their ever-changing reality while traversing the unfamiliarity of my own. I make a conscious decision to forego a formal job for the first time in my life for several reasons, foremost being the fragile state of my father. Meanwhile, as a committed Christian, I contend with questions and insecurity on account of my church life because I do not currently belong to a certain congregation, at least not one that I can point to with a specific name and address.

I had a church that I loved. I also had a full-time job that I sincerely enjoyed which happened to be at the church. I considered myself privileged to be a part of the congregation as well as the staff. But after working there a few years, my line of sight somehow grew wider, altering my previously held perspectives. What began as questions in my heart resulted in doubts that could not be resolved. I was not uncertain about Jesus or my Christianity, but about the church in which I was involved and its direction in relation to God's.

In time, I left the church and my job there just as surprisingly as I had arrived. After all, working at a church had not been some long-held aspiration. Growing up, I never thought of church as being particularly good or bad, enjoyable or not; I was simply made to go. In childhood, Mom had been Catholic and Dad was Methodist. After marrying, I suppose my parents saw the Presbyterian Church as some sort of meeting in the middle.

My childhood church was located on a long, wide boulevard not far from our house and was the backdrop of many sabbath mornings, though few I can remember.

I was expected to go to church weekly, and for the most part, I didn't mind going. However, I did not readily recall much from those Sunday services. One Sunday morning I do remember vividly. As my family prepared to go to church, I lied and told my mom that I was too sick with a stomachache to go. Dad stayed home with me that Sunday while Mom attended the service. After she returned and changed into casual attire, I told her I wanted to invite a friend to go outside and play. I was promptly told that my illness kept me from church and that it would also keep me from playing–at least for a few hours.

As a child raised in church, I failed to see that faith in God was intended to be consequential to daily living. And while I memorized everything necessary to be confirmed in my childhood church, I missed Jesus as my personal Savior. I memorized concepts, answered questions aloud before leadership, and was accepted on the congregation's roster. Still, I did not grasp biblical truths at a soul level. So in my teenage years, I became a denominational church member according to a list in the church office, but I was not a Christian.

I continued to attend church post-confirmation; meanwhile, God began to woo me outside of it. In high school, a friend invited me to a week-long summer camp, and I agreed to join her not knowing the camp was overtly Christian. Once there, I enjoyed the songs and speakers at the camp a great deal. Even more, the warm and kind nature of the camp counselor assigned to my cabin impacted me in a great way.

Walking across the field together one day, the boombox she was carrying fell to the ground while its handle remained tightly in her grasp. Seeing the radio crash to the ground, I anticipated her annoyed and angry response. Instead, I was shocked as I watched my counselor look up and let out a large belly laugh. *That's strange*, I thought, seeing her reaction as odd. If the same thing had happened to me, I knew I would have been irritated.

Throughout the week at camp, I was touched by my

counselor's disposition and the biblical messages I heard, but the truth of Christianity escaped my heart, going over my head. When my camp counselor asked how long I had been a Christian in a private moment together, I remember telling her, "My whole life." I thought I had been born into Christianity, just as I was Italian, because my maternal grandmother was. I didn't comprehend that my faith required a decision, one likely made at a specific moment in time.

About a year later, I more clearly understood that my beliefs were to be personal and not familial, chosen not inherited. In the spring of my junior year, a fellow student from my English class invited me to spend some time together one afternoon. Sitting across a table from him, I heard and understood the gospel plainly and simply: I was a sinner in need of a Savior. I came home, retreated to my room and prayed at the foot of my bed. Acknowledging I was a sinful person, I asked Jesus to forgive me of my sins and invited Him to become the Lord of my life.

I accepted Jesus at the end of my junior year in high school. Because I would move to a college campus before long, I remained part of the church I grew up in, mostly coasting in my faith for the remaining days of high school. I read the Bible (at least a little) and continued to attend church services on the weekends, but I wasn't exactly sure how to carry out a Christian life. I just knew I was heaven-bound and "saved" on account of Christ's death and resurrection, his triumph over my sin, and I recognized that I had a sincere desire to know and love Him more.

Before I began my freshman year of college, I joined a host of incoming classmates as part of a three-day orientation. Though I remember very few things about the experience, I do recall watching and listening as a handful of older students shared about a variety of organizations on campus. One of them stood up and gave some statistics about young adults and religion.

The upper-class student addressed those in the audience and explained that many college students fall away from their faith backgrounds, relinquishing the beliefs in which they were raised. He caught my attention as he went on to say, "We don't need more Christians. We don't need more Hindus. We don't need more Muslims. We need more people who will take the time to seek the truth about life, death, and God." His words struck me. While he had not petitioned those of us listening towards any particular faith, his mere admonishment caused me to more fully commit to the beliefs I had adopted the year before. Through quick observation, I noted the best-attended Christian fellowship on campus and promptly joined that group.

The sizeable chapter of College Christians United (CCU) and the God-fearing students that were part of it at my university left a deep and lasting impression on me. As I brushed shoulders with CCU students, I began to realize something was different between my Christianity and theirs. I was ethical and straitlaced. They were ethical, but they were also *different*. I observed that somehow, they appeared to live and relate to others from a place greater than a moral compass. I naturally wanted to spend time with them, recognizing they were unusually kind and authentic. Moreover, my heart wanted to emulate their lives as I observed how earnestly and consistently they lived out their faith.

Meanwhile, my understanding of Christianity and church was regularly challenged. During my first few weeks living in the dorms, a freshman friend asked me about the kind of congregation in which I was raised. When I told him *Presbyterian,* he barely took a breath and asked, "PCA or PCUSA?". I was stupefied by his question, not knowing there were different types of Presbyterian churches. Half troubled and half embarrassed, I sheepishly responded, "I have no idea."

I continued to absorb information about the Christian way of life during my first months on campus, and I also joined a mid-week Bible study in my dormitory. Along with participating in CCU, I snagged rides from older classmates and visited a few Christian congregations in the area. One Sunday morning, I grabbed a ride to a church I had never visited, feeling intrigued about the chance to go since I had heard great things about its worship services from several other students.

We rode to the church service in an old, white SUV that I

think was a Bronco, while I sat in the back and made friendly conversation with the driver. She was an outgoing blonde who was a fellow member of CCU, and she sported a rubber bracelet with the letters "WWJD" on it. I had no idea what that meant, and when I asked her, she excitedly explained that the acronym stood for: *What Would Jesus Do?*

Her bracelet left an impression on me that morning, and so did the church service we attended. The worship gathering was one I especially liked, and it seemed nothing like the services I experienced in my childhood. It was a "reformed" church, whatever that was. All I knew was that the pastor spoke with love, passion, and a personal relevance I had never witnessed before. I sincerely enjoyed my experience at the church and attended it quite consistently throughout my college years.

I felt increasingly secure in my faith, but confidence in my life's direction waned. During the first week of my senior year, I sat in a teaching practicum and realized how uncertain I felt about my major, strongly doubting that I wanted to become a high school teacher. Within a day, I met with my advisor and changed my major to a general degree, one that allowed me to graduate at the end of the school year. I was not sure what I wanted to do with my life, but I reasoned that I would hone a new direction following graduation instead of figure one out by prolonging an ambiguous and costly education.

Holding my Bachelor of Arts degree, I left my parents' house and the cold, gray Midwest weather with a resolute heart. I was determined to find a job in a milder climate, so I relocated to a sprawling and sizeable city, one situated several hundred miles south of my childhood home. New Haven was the place I chose to settle, a city surrounded by lush green trees and located within a much broader area commonly referred to as the Bible Belt.

I found a room for rent and moved into a small house with a single, middle-aged woman. I immediately contacted a host of temporary agencies and made appointments to meet with several of them. GPS did not exist, and I got lost more than once, wholly frustrated and bewildered that a single street could change names arbitrarily as I traveled on it. After successfully registering with a few agencies, I began accepting work for short-term job opportunities, mostly doing administrative tasks. Overall, I found the assignments to be enjoyable, even though I usually stayed at a given job for just a day or two at a time.

After a handful of weeks in my new surroundings, I began to settle into New Haven quite well. I still experienced moments where I felt overcome by stress and loneliness, and sometimes I cried. Securing a job as an Inside Sales Representative gave my morale a boost, and the permanent position led me to replace my temporary air mattress. Significant parts of my life began falling into place, and the resulting satisfaction kept me from returning to my roots.

Though I moved to New Haven largely on account of its warmer weather, I also imagined my recently adopted Christianity would naturally flourish there. Growing more comfortable in my new city, I began to feel empowered in my faith. I had the sole responsibility of picking a church, and in New Haven the possibilities seemed endless. I was far enough removed in years that the experiences from my childhood congregation felt irrelevant. Meanwhile, the church I attended in college resonated in my mind; it had left a significant impression on me concerning my concept of church and set the bar for the type of "flavor" I would seek. I was eager to find a local congregation upon moving and immediately started looking. Because the area had so many churches, I assumed I would like several that I visited and would simply have to pick one. I was wrong.

I visited a host of congregations, yet nothing seemed to fit. Over time, my search felt frustrating and somewhat hopeless. No church experience or message from the pulpit really *did it* for me. I attended several churches in a six-month stretch, eventually following a friend to a congregation thirty minutes outside our growing metropolis. Christian Community Fellowship (CCF) felt entirely different from my childhood church and surprisingly unlike the church I attended in college. But somehow, the small congregation outside the city limits drew me in. I continued to visit CCF, and in time it naturally became my new church home.

The modest church on the outskirts of town was made up of earnest people. Sunday mornings had a new and different feel than I had previously experienced within a congregation. Each weekend that I visited, I came to better understand the word *charismatic;* it felt like a fitting description of the church members as they expressively sang hymns and contemporary songs. The atmosphere in the sanctuary felt particularly free as people appeared quite relaxed and less rigid than I had historically observed during church services.

As the congregation sang, people clapped their hands, closed their eyes, and some swayed while raising their arms in the air. I felt an equal sense of surprise at witnessing the expressive movements and the fact that I did not find them distracting. Then, after a more ample time of singing each week than I was accustomed, the pastor paced side-to-side at the front of the sanctuary, carried a microphone, and spoke emphatically from the Bible. The atmosphere was unfamiliar and the preaching did not especially tickle my intellect each week. However, I loved the church and continued to attend because its members were genuine and quickly grew to feel like family.

In the church of about seventy, we were not fancy. The pastor did not have a city-wide reputation, and we were not readily growing in number. As far as churches go, I suppose CCF was relatively unknown. However, those inside the church were very well acquainted, and that's why I loved it. If the congregation in college was the first church where I heard relevant biblical teaching, CCF was the first church I felt truly known and loved. I attended the church for four years, only leaving because I moved to a new apartment. My new home was forty-five minutes away, a longer distance than seemed reasonable to drive for weekend worship services and mid-week events.

Years passed. I visited a host of churches but primarily attended four congregations in the first ten years I lived in New Haven. Each church I attended preserved the integrity of the Bible, played Christ-centered music and had worship services that felt welcoming. While every congregation was nice in its own right, I did not stay at any one of them for very long.

Though possibly pegged as a church-hopper, I finally settled into a congregation more long-term after finding the greatest church in New Haven.

I didn't know that a "greatest church" in the city existed, that is, until several people started telling me. With each passing year, I met more and more people who were a part of one particular local congregation. Intrigued, I eventually decided to pay Fairview Church a visit.

The day I attended Fairview for the first time, I elected to go to one of their afternoon services. As I walked down a row to find a seat, I took note of my surroundings and the varied impressions they left on me. Attending alone, I surveyed the people around me before the service began. The crowd was notably young, a striking observation since I was barely over thirty. I chose a seat towards the back and as the service progressed, I absorbed the experience while also trying to understand how the church had developed such a following. As the hour drew to a close and I got up to leave, I definitely didn't get it. In my opinion, the visit to Fairview Church had been *ok*, but the experience had not been something to write home about.

The church's sanctuary was industrial in nature and quite large. Attending church services in commercial spaces was not an unfamiliar experience, but the building had not been overly occupied during the service. As a result, the environment struck me as a bit empty and void of life. The demographics also left me feeling a bit odd, since the sparse crowd lacked people who were middle-aged and older. Overall, the visit left me wanting, but it also left me wondering. I had heard from many people about how great Fairview's pastor was, but his sermon didn't impress me because I was distracted by the fact that he preached at a decibel which made me feel as if he was yelling.

I did not get all the hype about Fairview Church at first, but a year following my first visit, I became a faithful visitor. After meeting a nice fellow and dating him for a few months, my boyfriend and I agreed to forego our respective congregations, intent on finding a new church that we could attend together. We visited Fairview Church and decided to make it our own.

Six months later, I remained at the church after the dating relationship ended and my ex moved out-of-state.

By that time, I had come to understand why others had been so emphatic about the church. It maintained phenomenal teaching, great worship music, and it had a large and established small group ministry. The congregation was also well-regarded in the city because of its community outreach.

I knew Fairview Church was a decent size, but I had no idea that New Haven had any megachurches. I didn't know what a *megachurch* was exactly, nor fully understood that I was sitting in one.

Chapter 2

KNOCKED DOWN, NOT OUT

When life kicks you, let it kick you forward.

Kay Yow

My concept of a megachurch was a vague one, and it came from Texas. A childhood friend, Heidi, relocated to the Dallas area after college, and I occasionally went to visit her. When she settled into her new city, a neighbor from her apartment complex invited her to church. Soon after, my friend became a Christian.

Jumping into her new Christian life, Heidi regularly talked about being involved with the singles group and the opportunities to serve in her congregation. I figured out quickly that her church was sizable and quite prominent in her city. I saw the church with my own eyes the next time I went to visit her.

The church campus that Heidi attended was large, and the building itself was sprawling. In my estimation, the sanctuary seated a few thousand people. I surveyed the church, walked through the wide halls, peered at the multi-tiered sanctuary, and stopped for a bit in the resource shop. I scanned the aisles and observed Bibles, journals and bookmarks for sale, even spotting something that looked like a diet or healthy living book written by her pastor. I had never seen anything like it. If there ever was a megachurch, her church was one.

Back home at Fairview Church, the Sunday service I frequented held a few hundred people. Because I was attending one of the satellite campuses, the church did not feel nearly as large as my friend's church in Texas, and I had no idea that her congregation and mine were remotely comparable. In time, I understood that Fairview Church was, in fact, a megachurch. It had several campuses and thousands of attendees. It was also rapidly growing. A few campus locations met on Saturdays, and some held as many as five worship services on the weekends.

Choosing to join the church was a slow process for me, largely because Fairview had several characteristics that I never expected in a church I might call home. As I sought a new church body, I did anticipate choosing one with solid teaching and wonderful worship music, two qualities that were true of Fairview Church. However, I never planned to attend a church with thousands of people and multiple campuses, where most congregants would watch the pastor projected onto a screen. The size alone caused certain questions to surface in my mind and also contributed to an underlying sense of skepticism I had about the church. *Why can't they stay in one place and leave some of the city for other churches in the area, rather than take-over so much of New Haven?* I wondered.

My questions and concerns were ultimately answered upon going to an informational meeting intended for potential new members. I visited the church for a year before attending the meeting, feeling persuaded to go after listening to the words of a Fairview pastor one weekend and taking them to heart. He addressed the congregation during a normal worship service and expressed the importance of church membership in every Christ follower's life.

At the new membership class, I started to comprehend the overarching heart and philosophy of the church. I also better understood the reason behind their many campuses. A large number of congregants drove significant distances, bypassing other local churches on the way to Fairview Church. Since congregants were committed to attend the church and were driving substantial distances to do so, Fairview had chosen to create smaller, cheaper satellite campuses in the areas where their commuting congregants lived.

After hearing Fairview Church's history and ideology, I came to accept the congregation's large size. In turn, I felt more comfortable about deciding to make the church my home. So after one year of visiting and attending the new members class, I spoke with an elder and became an official member of Fairview Church. I was committed to it and would remain there for several years to come.

During my membership at Fairview, my Christianity deepened by way of knowledge and experience. Each week, I was on the receiving end of rich and substantial sermons, ones that consistently provoked my heart and challenged my thinking. Meanwhile, daily circumstances tested my faith and exposed weaknesses as I tried to follow Jesus in the ups, downs, and unexpected things in life.

At the time I joined Fairview Church, I was in my early thirties. My closest friends were happily married, though I found myself only desperately wishing to be. I had long borne witness to bridal showers, weddings, baby showers and subsequent birthdays. I wanted to rejoice in the many happy occasions, but I experienced an ever-encroaching sadness. The reasons to celebrate were always someone else's. I held onto hope that God would bring me a husband, but his timing felt unusually slow. The delay felt unwarranted, and it deeply hurt my heart.

As a result, I sometimes doubted God's love for me, and my feelings occasionally morphed into cynicism. Given my age, I assumed a future wedding, if I were to have one, would be a second marriage for my husband, thus second-rate for me. As my frustration with God's timing ebbed and flowed, so did my romantic life. I dated a few people I should not have and became more physically involved with them than I ought. In seeking companionship, romantic-fulfillment and fun, I was bold to take for myself what God seemed unwilling to give me. I felt bad about my behavior but also justified; the wait for wedded bliss simply felt too long.

Though I engaged in a tug of war with God concerning my

circumstances, I still sought to follow him while I continued to attend Fairview faithfully. Meanwhile, the Lord began speaking to me very clearly about foster care. Over the course of a year, God nudged my soul and conscience repeatedly, urging me to become a foster parent. About the time I acknowledged that God's promptings were irrefutable, I took a road trip and drove with my mouth agape as I passed a billboard that read, "Become a Foster Parent Today." It was a sign I had never seen, though I was hardly a stranger to the expressway it marked.

God's message to me about fostering was unrelenting. I was as certain about God's call as I was sure he had dialed the wrong person. Frankly, I had virtually no experience with children. The youngest of two, I "babysat" most often for one child in my neighborhood, a certain boy nearly old enough to stay at home by himself. In "babysitting" him, I functioned far more as an older friend or companion than some responsible and competent caregiver.

Wholly uncomfortable with God's directive to foster and yet being certain of it, I moved forward with the necessary training and chose to pursue my certification through the county. Truthfully, I assumed the Lord would never actually place a child into my care before putting a future husband in my life because if he allowed that to happen, God would be undeniably crazy. A year later, I stood in my foyer and shed tears in a wave of shock and disbelief as I realized the foster certification paperwork arrived, yet no marital prospect had.

Meanwhile, during several months of the training process, I hid my intent to foster from my parents. Though loving and charitable people, I knew my mom and dad would have opinions that ran contrary to my choice. I kept my decision under wraps, feeling certain they would heartily object because of the complexity involved in caring for a traumatized child. Already maintaining a measure of fear in my decision, I wanted to guard against concern or disapproval from anyone else, particularly from the individuals I loved and respected most.

Normally, I would have experienced an epic failure in trying to keep such a secret from my mother who happens to be my best friend, but waiting to tell her the news was actually never an issue. At the time I embarked on foster training classes, the same month I would have been inclined to leak the news, my family was struck by an all-encompassing crisis that hijacked life as we knew it.

Leveled to the floor by a mysterious pain in his neck, my dad was admitted to a major medical hospital not far from my parents' home. Misdiagnosed, his illness went untreated for days though doctors and nurses circled his bed. He writhed in excruciating pain for a week before his condition was accurately assessed. A staph infection had overtaken his body, and the delay in proper treatment resulted in his near-death.

During the long weeks in the hospital, a few friends visited Dad while others placed meals on our porch because someone was rarely home to receive them. Food that had been prepared with care was often consumed standing in the kitchen late at night, or it was put immediately in the fridge as each of us fell into bed, too exhausted to eat.

Though Dad lived, my family was forced to survive the devastating debacle with him, bearing witness to resuscitations and procedures during his 9-week hospital stay. He was eventually transferred from the hospital to a rehabilitation facility, but his ultimate discharge home felt like a nightmare instead of a dream.

The complications in caring for my father were beyond overwhelming for my mother, brother and me. Collateral damage was unavoidable as we all attempted to cope, ill-equipped to do anything except drag ourselves through each day, ever desperate for a better one. Dad's care required constant physical and emotional energy, resources that seemed long depleted from the few of us who were left to care for him.

The medical mistake never paid out a penny except, I suppose, in large dividends chalked up to greater "life experience"—experience we never wanted. Complications from the fiasco never ceased, but at least the most critical days and moments did. We managed to get to the other side of the all-encompassing months, thankful to have Dad with us, but we also faced the fact that future hardships were inevitable for all of us due to his hugely compromised health.

Then, with my family's life becoming a little calmer, I finally felt the time was slightly suitable to disclose my intent to become foster certified. I gently dropped the bomb to my parents and brother over a low-key pizza dinner. "I know this is going to come as a surprise, but I am going to be a foster parent," I casually announced, then braced myself for expected rebuttals.

"Don't call me if you need help," my brother blurted. I smirked, looking immediately back at my parents. Coming face-to-face with their hesitations about foster care was no surprise and affirmed that withholding my decision from them was wise. Because I was miraculously able to complete the classroom portion of the certification in the months coinciding my family's crisis, mom and dad seemed to respect my resolve and kept their outward concerns to a minimum.

Life continued to level out for all of us. Over the next many months, my parents adjusted to Dad's impairments and limitations. I completed the secondary steps to be foster certified and began my active wait, imperfectly poised to receive my first placement. A novice with children, no matter the age, I asked my social worker for a female child, eight-years-old or older.

Though some onlookers wondered why I would elect to take an older child, I had chosen an age range that terrified me least. I hoped to have a smidgen of competency with a child that I could converse and reason with, but my reasoning flew out the window before the year drew to a close. Just before Christmas, I received my first foster placement only to find myself waving a big white flag shortly thereafter.

A deeply hurting teen, Jamie was a "classic" foster child. She came to my home on a Friday afternoon, hours after I learned about her, without any personal belongings apart from the clothes she was wearing. Going to Target the next morning, we easily exhausted the voucher given to us by the county, securing new clothing and a pair of shoes. After a textbook "honeymoon" period with peace reigning in our home and relationship, the façade of our earnest connection eroded.

Every day after school, Jamie indicated she had no

homework—a story I wholeheartedly believed. Since Jamie was repeating the sixth grade, I naively assumed she was mastering the familiar concepts quickly. Weeks later, about the same time she began running away (and throwing tantrums as well as household items), I discovered she had been given homework regularly but never completed it. Despite meeting with her teachers and increasing her accountability at home, Jamie's needs surpassed my ability to meet them.

Less than three months from the day Jamie entered my life, I asked my social worker to place the troubled young girl of thirteen with a new foster family. Having been traumatized by my experience with such a deeply hurting teen, I took a six-month hiatus before permitting my social worker to place me on the "active" list to receive another placement. She called me several weeks later—sooner than I had hoped—regarding a new placement, a fourteen-year-old. Amber moved in days later and quickly showed herself to be kind and bright.

Amber and I were still adjusting to one another and life together when, just after the New Year, a friend set me up on a blind date–one she orchestrated against my will. However, her hunch to introduce me to a coworker proved divine. Steve and I were a perfect match and married four months after our first date. I turned thirty-six a few weeks later, more time than I needed to know the wait for Mr. Right was worth the heartache I had felt for so long.

Steve, Amber and I started to find our groove together as a new, though somewhat a-typical family, even settling into a more sizeable home before Christmas. Having jumped on the fast-track to foster certification before exchanging vows, Steve dove head-first with me into marriage and parenting.

I felt grateful. Life finally felt a bit more balanced. With each passing day, Steve ever proved to be my best friend, and as we approached the one-year anniversary of when she was placed in my care, Amber continued to warm-up to us both. Having a few mountains of hardship behind, I felt eager and anticipated more happy days ahead.

Chapter 3

THE GOLDEN TICKET

Mr. Wonka: "Don't forget what happened to the man who suddenly got everything he wanted."
Charlie Bucket: "What happened?"
Mr. Wonka: "He lived happily ever after."

Willy Wonka and the Chocolate Factory

As Steve and I adjusted to life together, attending Fairview Church continued to be a positive experience in our Christian faith as a newly married couple. Though he had been raised in a much more traditional church, Steve and I decided to attend Fairview after we married, partially motivated by the budding faith of our foster daughter. When Amber was placed in my care, she joined me for a few services at Fairview. About the time that Steve entered our lives, she had started showing curiosity, asking Steve and me questions about Jesus. Because the church appeared to be a catalyst in her growing faith, we felt that remaining at Fairview was wise.

Steve was new to the church and all it offered, but I had attended long enough to be involved in different opportunities there. As a single person at the church, I had taken part in a small group and volunteered in a few different capacities during services. I attended the campus night celebrations and women's gatherings and participated in a 1-on-1 study with a more mature and wiser woman. Together, the experiences created a church life that was truly full.

Recognizing my growing attachment to Fairview and knowing how insecure I felt at my current place of employment, Steve looked at me one day and said, "You should look for a job at the church." "A job at the church?" I said, "Ha! That would never happen." I appreciated Steve's suggestion and apparent vote of confidence, but I did not take him seriously.

Landing a job at Fairview Church would be a dream–one I never let myself have. I felt there was no sense dreaming about something that would never come to pass. I imagined every one of the 10,000 attendees would love to work at the church, so I deemed it an impossibility, if only by probability. I dismissed Steve's suggestion and quickly forgot his remark.

A few months later, Steve and I felt it was time to emerge from our newlywed life. We had lived quietly cloistered for the first few months of marriage. Having enjoyed some extended time together, we were ready to branch out in our new life as a couple. We agreed that one of the ways we wanted to foster our faith was by joining a small group through the church. So one weekend afternoon at Steve's prompting, I sat on the couch with my laptop and navigated to the *Small Groups* page of Fairview's website.

I scanned the information about small groups and how to connect to one. Then, at the very bottom of the page, my eyes naturally skimmed over an unrelated link. I had not been looking for it, but right in the middle of the page was a link to job openings at the church. With equal hesitation and curiosity, I clicked on it.

As the page opened, I saw a few positions listed and, to my surprise, a job for an administrative assistant was among them. Though I currently worked in Human Resources, the job description was similar to a few administrative positions I previously held, and the role was surely in my realm of interest. I knew the odds of getting the job were low, but I decided to apply. I located the last version of my resume and diligently but swiftly updated it. After typing out my answers to the on-line questions, I uploaded my resume, took a breath, and hit *submit*.

I felt no surprise when I did not get a call that week. However, the lull of normal life took an abrupt turn a week or so later when I actually did get a call. With my cell phone ringing, I stepped away from my cubicle at work and slid into a small, unoccupied conference room. I talked to the hiring manager long enough to answer a few basic questions and, before hanging up, inquired a bit more about the position.

The manager indicated that the administrative position I had applied for had been filled. Immediately perplexed, I asked him why he was calling me if the position was no longer available. He explained that he was just getting ready to hire someone for a full-time Human Resources role but had not posted the position yet. Upon receiving my application, he saw that my current job was in HR and thought I might be a good fit. As he explained the situation, I became increasingly excited; HR was my current line of work, and the new role would largely parallel my current position and job knowledge.

On the day of the in-person interview, I found myself unexpectedly driving my husband's car. As the interview came to a close, I returned to the car and observed Cheerios (my husband's snack of choice) lining the driver's seat. I turned around and sighed as I surveyed the crumbs on the back side of my black business skirt. Momentarily mortified, I shrugged it off and told myself the interview went well because I believed it had.

Within a day, my feeling was confirmed as an offer letter landed in my inbox. Upon opening the email, I flew through the hallway in happy disbelief and ran down the stairs to find Steve. It was official–I was the recipient of a rare opportunity to join a sizeable church staff of over 100 full-time employees. I would be the newest member of a broad range of professionals, one that supported a phenomenal church body, and I was going to be paid to have this awesome honor.

I had been a Christian for well-over ten years, but an especially sweet season in my walk with God was commencing. I was ecstatic to become increasingly enveloped in my Christian faith, working for the beloved congregation in which I was a part.

Chapter 4

A TILTED HEAD

Cleave ever to the sunnier side of doubt.

Alfred, Lord Tennyson

Leaving my old job in order to assume my new position at Fairview Church was a no-brainer; returning for the second day at my new job was not. I received only a few hours of training based on the availability of the woman I was replacing. She had worked in the position on a part-time basis and elected not to maintain it as it grew to a full-time role. Despite the limited training I received, I was thankful that the former position I had just left was incredibly similar to my new job at Fairview. As a result, the learning curve felt like it would be short. However, within the first day, I realized I would have a bigger adjustment to my new job than I had anticipated.

First, the position would require me to run payroll, something I had never done before. The previous company I worked for was much larger, thus the employees within the HR department had been much more siloed. In my new role, with the total employee base being so much smaller, I would wear more hats within HR than I had in my last position. Running payroll was not difficult, except being privy to the information I managed. I processed payroll through a web-based program while inadvertently pondering some of the numbers I saw.

Handling proprietary data was not new to me. Functioning as a Benefits Administrator at my previous employer, I had access to all salaries and managed sensitive information daily. Working for the church was just a fresh context to handle people's income, knowing that the giving of others supported what the staff members earned.

Upon leaving the office on my first day, my husband and I converged at home and he greeted me with bells on, standing in our bedroom. I entered his embrace and fell apart, crying. Not knowing what was wrong, Steve was surprised and concerned. When I expressed skepticism and a sense of worry as I disclosed the lead pastor's rate of pay, he was non-reactionary and immediately replied in a manner to put my mind at ease.

"To be honest," he said, "I'm somewhat surprised he's not paid more." *"Really?"* I said, still unsure. Steve was not overly fazed at what I had shared and encouraged me to look at the size of Fairview's congregation. While it was a different kind of institution, the church had employees, salaries and revenue, not unlike a business. Steve pointed out that in successful corporations, ones comparable to the size of Fairview, many CEOs would be earning much, much more.

I stood opposite of Steve and cautiously absorbed his words. Considering the number of attendees at Fairview and the corresponding scope of responsibility, Steve's reasoning seemed to make sense. He continued to comfort my conscience, sharing that when his parents' small church had last hired a pastor, his salary was a source of contention for at least a few within the congregation.

I was thankful for Steve's objectivity which helped take the edge off of my anxiousness. Even so, his response did not dispel my sense of concern completely. As we closed our conversation, I still felt a bit shocked by his lack of surprise, but one of the qualities that drew me to marry Steve was his ability to seek reason in difficult situations while remaining level-headed.

As we hugged and changed into casual attire, I strangely suspected my husband's manner of approach was one I should more readily adapt. After talking to Steve, I became aware that it would behoove me to examine things from different angles as I continued to learn the responsibilities of my new role. My guard had gone up on the first day, but I realized I may have been overreacting. In the future, I would aim to look at the information that I handled in a more distant fashion in order to assume a proper perspective.

The resolve to dial back my reactions served me well, as my unrest surrounding the pastor's compensation was not the last concern I would have. Each month upon paying the staff's retirement invoice, I had trouble reconciling my conscience concerning the amount being spent on our staff members' 403(b). I felt surprised and a bit guilty about my newly formed qualms with the benefit because at the time I was hired, the retirement plan was outlined in my offer letter and I had felt it was attractive while not being wholly outside of reason.

After one year of employment, the church would contribute 5% of my annual salary to a 403(b), regardless if I personally chose to contribute; additionally, Fairview would match up to 5% if I did elect to personally participate. In essence, the church gave me an additional 10% of my annual salary towards retirement, a whopping and unprecedented amount. No vesting date existed for the benefit, so the monies would be fully mine no matter when I might leave employment at Fairview. Though the employer contribution and matching were more than I had ever heard of before, I felt the church was seeking to be fair in my overall compensation, especially since I was taking a $10,000 pay cut upon accepting the position.

Somehow, from the time I accepted the HR job at Fairview to the first month I assumed its responsibilities, my perspective changed. Before, I saw the retirement benefit as being rich but not exorbitant, all things considered. However, upon sitting in my role, questions about the retirement benefit inadvertently bubbled up as I observed the sum being spent each month. I earnestly wondered if the benefit was sustainable and whether the employer portion of the contribution was truly "right" regardless. Though my concerns over the benefit would never fully go away, I regularly reasoned that it had been in place before I arrived and apparently ignited no sense of alarm in those seated above me.

As I continued in my job, I questioned certain pieces of

information I was exposed to but learned to look at the new and sometimes uncomfortable knowledge from different angles. I wanted to be certain that I considered the whole picture of each situation before succumbing to automatic judgments. Meanwhile, I had been informed upon hire that Fairview's employees would soon be traveling out of town, headed a few hours away for an annual staff retreat. *A retreat?* I wondered. In my previous jobs, I had the privilege of doing some event planning. Without a doubt, I had fun planning special events and taking part in them, but my thoughts instinctively focused on the fact that they were undoubtedly costly.

    I immediately felt hesitant about the event because I knew there would be lost productivity during the time we were away; additionally, I had concerns about the cost of the retreat itself. However, I reasoned that the church was seeking to love its employees, wanting to care for us well as so few corporations do. Besides, we would be staying at a retreat center and receiving a significant discount, apparently on account of the denomination Fairview was affiliated. Suspending any judgement, I left for the retreat feeling skeptical about its costs and benefits, but I was curious whether my apprehensions would last.

    Upon going to the retreat and having a wonderful time, I returned feeling it was a good investment. My perspectives about the staff's allotted time together, away from New Haven and our normal office duties, changed so much that I wrote a card to one of Fairview's leaders about our off-site experience. In the note, I expressed my initial skepticism about the retreat and then explained how I ultimately valued the time; finally, I closed my hand-written card by extending gratitude for the opportunity we had been given.

    The retreat was one more benefit of being a staff member that I could see from many different points of view. I felt honored to receive unusual perks, but they inevitably resulted in gratitude mixed with guilt. The staff culture was generous and gracious, but as I grew familiar with its inner workings, our workplace decreasingly resembled most "normal" ones. My internal conflict was heightened when, because of my position,

I was involved with facilitating certain benefits I believed were unwarranted or lavish. For instance, at management's initiative, full-time workers were given additional days off during the summer months, and I was responsible for making the announcement. Posting the news on the staff's message board was difficult, knowing I did not agree with the arbitrary days off, especially in light of Fairview's already generous policies (e.g. days off for illness, PTO, professional ministry opportunities, and volunteerism).

Apart from daily operations that grew familiar, I sometimes inadvertently learned new information that troubled me. Paying invoices was commonplace, and I processed several of them for benefits, like monthly medical premiums. But periodically, I indirectly learned about services or products that caused me concern. For example, well before I joined Fairview's staff, I had participated with other congregants in a church-wide campaign. After I became an employee, the congregation embarked on a new one. The campaign slogans were short, catchy, and encouraged each congregant toward a "sold out" life for God. Through them, parishioners were implored to give God their best—in time, talents, prayer, and money. Shock came over me when I happened to learn the campaigns were managed by a third-party. We had many creative, competent, and paid people on our staff. Knowing we outsourced such a "project" was disheartening, but I was dumbstruck upon hearing a portion of its price tag. The knowledge left me feeling icky, as if the church was using congregants' financial gifts to hire professionals for the purpose of obtaining more money from the same people—me included.

With each new experience I took part in or business practice I witnessed, I learned that I could question certain things or elect to hold confidence in those managing them. Still, reconciling thoughts about different situations was not a rare occurrence, and I did not always understand scenarios outside of those specifically involving money.

For example, one of the positions within our staff was, in essence, a Researcher. Part of the role was to provide information that the lead pastor utilized for his work, like a sermon or blog. I thought that the job seemed odd because of its responsibility, and the fact that the person doing the research would hardly, if ever, be identified. However, I heard the role was not an unusual one, something confirmed when a friend of a friend was hired in a similar position at a church a few hours away. Upon learning about the job, I did not necessarily understand or agree with its function; then again, I figured that if other churches employed such a person, and the one doing the role did not mind working with little to no acknowledgment, who was I to question it.

Over time, doubts that I had about different issues did not slow nor altogether cease. I often made peace with one issue only to have another surface a little while later. In some ways, reasoning against my initial responses felt disingenuous to my conscience; in other ways, it seemed like the right thing to do. Many of Fairview's staff members had been part of the church for decades and were pillars within the congregation, leaders who had been present long enough to witness the church's resurgence after the installment of the current lead pastor. Though concerns about policies and processes surfaced in my mind quite regularly, I naturally reasoned that their decisions were best.

Observing certain practices left me feeling insecure, but I chose to concentrate on my personal scope of responsibility—accuracy and order in the data I maintained. Though I sometimes inquired with my manager about matters that troubled me, I resolved not to obsess over them. Instead, I felt relief they were not mine to own. A person who avoided managerial roles, I did not seek more responsibility for fear of accidentally mishandling it. As a result, whenever I encountered doubts or questions about the practices of Fairview Church, I naturally yielded to the wisdom of others, even if senior management did not pursue change or consider that it may be necessary.

I loved Fairview and wanted to live in a way that honored the staff's motto of sorts, to believe the best about fellow employees, something I was encouraged to do upon being hired. I appreciated the notion behind the words. I saw the principle as being a positive one that promoted a Christian heart in the workplace, a healthy and gracious attitude between workers, something altogether rare at most jobs. Additionally, before I accepted the position, my manager shared with me how the church and staff were not perfect so I should not expect working at Fairview would be either. I respected the wisdom he offered, and since I had accepted the position, his words had obviously not created alarm, as if he was bursting some idyllic bubble I had about working there.

As I gained time under my belt as an employee, I enjoyed my job while trying not to take it for granted. Unlike some staff members, I had logged several years in Corporate America, so I knew the culture at Fairview was considerably better than the "real world." While I was thankful for the chance I had been given to work there, I sometimes felt guilty. Being an employee at Fairview was an experience I was certain many would love to have, so I often pondered why I had been among the few that were afforded the opportunity. Recognizing I would never have the answer, whenever my mind wandered that way, I tried to turn my questioning into deliberate thoughts of thanksgiving.

My sense of gratitude did not wane, and I often recognized that my life's circumstances were especially good. I had a job I really liked and was part of a staff that I genuinely admired. I enjoyed working as a staff member so much that I sometimes caught myself wondering if I would ever leave my employment at Fairview. I knew God could always instigate change in my life, but I could not help but consider the possibility of remaining at Fairview until retirement.

Being a member and employee of such a landmark church was an indescribable blessing, something grand and seemingly sacred. My heart was wholly invested in Fairview, both as my place of worship and as my place of employment. I felt as if I had a front row seat to watch God's activity in and through our congregation; meanwhile, I felt a sense of anticipation concerning it and naturally wondered what the Lord would do next.

Chapter 5

A COSTLY DECISION

The only victories which leave no regret are those which are gained over ignorance.

Napoleon Bonaparte

Being one of the fastest growing churches in the nation, one of our seemingly consistent issues was a lack of seating. Usually, we remedied this by creating a new satellite campus. The leadership determined where a large pocket of our congregants lived then planted a new campus location there. The cost was low, relatively speaking, as we would establish a modest meeting place, usually in a school or other rented facility.

In time, our leadership approached us with a different kind of problem regarding capacity. Our main building, where our pastor spoke and most people attended, was not providing ample seating for the growth we were experiencing at that location. It was a different kind of issue. The main building would need to be addressed. Could we add on or restructure the walls in order to accommodate more people per service? We could, but engineers had already assessed the existing building and said remodeling would cost nearly as much as a new building while providing fewer additional seats.

The church's leadership team met to discuss their concern over capacity and together sought a solution. In the spring, the leaders brought their suggested remedy before the members of Fairview Church, a congregation of about 10,000. The written proposal recommended that the congregation borrow money to build a new and larger facility.

The proposed building would be located about 20 miles from the original broadcast location and would provide ample seating for old and new attendees. The more sizeable facility would also absorb all congregants from another nearby campus, one whose attendance hovered close to capacity and that would dissolve upon the new location opening. Meanwhile, Fairview would maintain ownership of its original broadcast location which would become a satellite campus, a location where congregants watched the pastor's sermon projected onto a screen.

Congregants listened as the information was laid out. An expansion plan was not a new idea to the church body. Members anticipated the church might build a new facility and had already started making plans for it. The previous summer, the church had voted in favor of securing an empty plot of land. The land was duly purchased and had been paid for in cash.* At the time the vote took place, a financial campaign was already underway, and portions of the financial gifts were intended for capital investments. With the land secured and the church's membership committed to ongoing giving, constructing a bigger building seemed like an obvious next step.

The financial requirements of the proposed project were outlined within the leaders' recommendation. In the written proposal, the congregation was reminded of Fairview Church's existing debt, about $17 million dollars. I sat in my seat and let the number sink in.

If the debt had been disclosed during the years of my membership, it was a number I had not remembered. Though a bit surprised, the amount of existing debt did not altogether shock me. After all, houses are rarely paid for in cash, even those for God's people to gather. And while the debt was certainly substantial, I strongly suspected it was not wholly abnormal for churches the size of Fairview.

---

*According to my recollection, the land had been paid for in cash. Our ability to pay for it directly and in-full had been a factor in my decision to vote in favor of the purchase, from what I recall.

Beyond laying out the amount we currently owed, the leaders' proposal recommended the congregation secure additional financing, not to exceed an extra $23 million dollars. The new loan would help cover the cost of constructing a larger broadcast building. If the congregation approved the leaders' recommendation, the projected total debt would increase to about $39.9 million dollars. While the debt was significant, leadership affirmed the solution before they presented it and believed the plan was fiscally responsible, well within the means of the church's overall budget.

Upon hearing the leaders' recommendation that weekend, each congregant also received written information concerning it. Parishioners were given a few pieces of paper outlining the recommendation to take home for further consideration and review. Meanwhile, the lead pastor shared various thoughts concerning the proposal by way of a brief video.

The impending congregational vote would follow in a few months, so members had that amount of time to understand and examine the implications of the recommendation before voting on it. Congregants were invited to ask questions and seek clarification during the weeks and months ahead. Meanwhile, the church had already established several avenues for them to do so. An email address was created specifically for parishioners to submit questions or to voice concerns, and leaders were designated to respond by email or meet with congregants as needed.

I left the service that day somewhat scratching my head, but I maintained respect for the option in front of us, even though I felt its delivery was sorely lacking. The information congregants received did not include the proposed terms of the new loan, should they vote to approve it. As a result, I wondered how I could vote on a loan without knowing approximately how long the church would be paying it off and the interest rate that the church would be charged.

Another observation that bothered me was rooted in the wording of the proposal and the delivery of the pastor's message in the video clip we watched. Both seemed to present the idea to the church body as if the decision had already been made. I was well aware that we had already secured the land with the anticipation of building on it, but upon being informed of the bottom line that day, I instinctively became hesitant. I suspected the congregation may need to press pause on our original plan of action to build and reassess the situation as a whole.

I also felt troubled because the financial numbers that had been presented to the congregation seemed huge, but I felt as if the leadership presented them in a manner which implied they were of little consequence. I naturally became unsure about the road ahead as I mulled over the numbers that I heard, but Fairview's leaders appeared undeterred. The leaders' motivation seemed to be rooted in a desire to see more people come to salvation through Jesus Christ, but I was overwhelmed to somehow find myself comparing the cost of a building with the cost of lost souls.

All in all, the proposal felt staggering. The way it had been communicated left me with questions, but the "correct" answer remained unclear in my mind. Just as I saw reasons to take pause and suspend our former plans, affirming the proposal seemed natural and favorable in other ways. First, the church had already executed some initial and significant steps in anticipating an expansion. Second, the recommended course of action had been extended to the congregation by the church's leaders.

Fairview's elders were specific individuals serving Fairview Church under the lordship of Christ. Every elder had been vetted, known by many within the body as mature in their Christian walk. Though our leaders were not known personally by everyone at Fairview Church on account of the congregation's size, parishioners were invited to get to know potential leaders before electing them. As a result, I was among a greater church body that was inclined to trust Fairview's leaders and the direction they deemed best, believing each elder to be a person of integrity, humble and God-fearing.

Finally, not voting to construct a larger meeting space seemed to risk potential growth of God's kingdom. Upon presenting their recommendation, leaders reminded us how

Fairview had always maintained a desire to see new people come to saving faith through Jesus Christ; additionally, the church had historically made choices proving that the growth of God's family was a priority. Without that resolve changing in our hearts, the proposed plan appeared to put us in a position to continue welcoming more individuals into God's fold, something I felt sure we wanted to do.

The impending vote was significant, and the information we were given was a lot to digest. As I left the church building that day, I felt the weightiness of the decision but maintained some sense of ease, knowing we had a substantial amount of time to explore the details of the recommended path before us. Though I was unsure what additional tools the leaders would give us to aid our decision making, I anticipated our elders equipping us with many.

Among them, I suspected Fairview's leaders would hold informational meetings, establish open forums for congregants to share knowledge and perspectives, and that our lead pastor would invite us into designated times of intercession so that we were certain to cover the decision in prayer. So long as we helped one another to be thoroughly informed and submitted to God's directive, I maintained confidence that within a few months, congregants would be well prepared to pick up their pencils and cast their votes.

Chapter 6

MOVE IN, OR MOVE OUT

There is a view of life which conceives that where the crowd is, there also is the truth. There is another view of life which conceives that wherever there is a crowd, there is untruth.

Soren Kierkegaard

Time moved swiftly, and week after week services passed normally. Meanwhile, conversations about the proposal were seemingly sparse. Though I observed discussions about the forthcoming decision to be nearly non-existent during my work days at the office, I regularly discussed the proposal at home with my husband. If the proposal were to pass, Steve and I shared concerns about the amount of debt the church would assume in addition to the interest involved in paying it off.

I sought to approach the corporate decision carefully, but privately I failed to understand why Fairview's leadership was resolved to remedy its capacity issues with a new building. Not meaning to belittle a legitimate concern of the church's leadership, I wondered why the lead pastor did not simply implore several church members at the broadcast location to shift their attendance to other locations indefinitely.

As our predominant leader, the pastor maintained an influential position, one where it would not be inappropriate for him to ask a portion of congregants to move to nearby campuses, locations with a greater number of empty seats. I suspected that for many congregants, changing campuses would only require an extra five or ten-minute drive. I also imagined that several parishioners would be willing to move and make a "sacrifice," knowing that their decision to change campuses would help alleviate crowding and create more seating at the broadcast location. I thought that if the church approached the issue in this manner, the problem would be fixed, at least for some time, essentially for free.

The idea to ease capacity by having congregants move to other locations came to my mind because it was very similar to one Fairview had already implemented at another campus successfully. In the satellite campus closest to my home, we had experienced crowding issues, especially on Sunday mornings. Though I was unaware a capacity issue had developed, our campus pastor explained the growing problem and urged us repeatedly to consider moving our attendance to the newly established Saturday service.

The pleadings of our campus pastor persuaded my conscience. I deferred to his request and changed my attendance to Saturday afternoons, hesitantly willing to try it for a time. Though I did not like attending church services on Saturday at the onset, I stayed long enough to be "sold" on the new time, even growing to prefer it. Apparently, the campus pastor convinced enough people, and the Sunday morning capacity issue eased. If the congregation's approach had ultimately worked for our satellite campus and had created vacant seats for new people, it seemed reasonable that the main facility could implement a similar solution.

Other times, I wondered why the leadership did not determine to solve the broadcast location's capacity issue by establishing a new satellite campus altogether. Instead of building a new, larger facility, it seemed plausible to me that Fairview could create an additional modest facility, even at a location close to the broadcast location. If they did, I imagined our pastor could implore a segment of the congregation to attend the nearby satellite campus instead of frequenting the location where the sermon was shared live each week. Had Fairview provided congregants with a new location and asked some members to move, I felt confident that many would be willing, and the capacity issue could be solved quite cheaply, relatively speaking.

Despite feeling there were more prudent ways to create additional seating for our current and future congregants, they were not solutions that had been presented to the congregation. Though I felt somewhat confused about why the church body had not been offered more options and that we did not discuss them earlier in the culmination of our capacity issue, I assumed leadership had examined the matter from many different angles. With our elders looking out for the church's overall well-being, I believed they had deduced that building a new facility was the "best" option for many reasons, even if I was not privy to them.

Therefore, I looked at the option facing the congregation and aimed to approach my vote responsibly. Leadership presented what they believed that God would have Fairview do, and I sought to know whether the Lord would have me agree. I spoke with my husband, crunched some numbers, and prayed regularly. Meanwhile, I waited.

Congregants had received handouts with some information on the day the proposal was presented, but significant details about the leaders' plan seemed dormant, waiting to be unearthed and better understood. Though Fairview's elders never indicated subsequent meetings would be held to further discuss the potential loan, I inadvertently assumed some would materialize in the months prior to our church-wide vote. Week after week, I attended worship services hoping additional information would be extended to the congregation, but I grew increasingly anxious when it was not.

The ongoing absence of follow-up meetings became a growing concern in my mind because it seemed to indicate a misstep in our approach, even one foreshadowing a potential mistake in our forthcoming decision. I did not want to discredit the parishioners' intelligence, but I felt unsure whether our church body was capable of managing the decision surrounding the elders' proposal wisely, especially if those leading us did not take intentional and increasing measures to unpack the implications of borrowing such a sum of money.

The closest comparison that I could think of to the sizeable decision we faced as a church body was home ownership. Well into my thirties, I was a home owner, something I was not sure to be true about most other congregants. Moreover, I had only applied for and closed on a home loan in a manner that I determined to be truly wise because others had helped me, foremost my parents. Considering my own decision to buy a home, I knew an array of factors were involved as well as many layers of data. Therefore, as our church body approached the exceedingly larger issue in front of us, I suspected each congregant brought a different measure of business savvy to aid our decision but imagined most of that knowledge was marginal.

On account of my age coupled with my experience in buying a home, I sometimes wondered if I was possibly among a smaller segment of the congregation, one slightly better equipped and more mindful about the decision we faced as a church. Even if I represented a portion of people that happened to be ahead of the general curve as far as being knowledgeable, the thought provided no sense of personal confidence as I approached my vote. Frankly, I feared not knowing certain information, data that might prove essential to arrive at the best decision; moreover, I felt inept in my ability to amass it, lest someone hand it to me.

The questions I had thought to pose were few which seemed to leave many more outstanding, ones I was not wise enough to ask. Assuming Fairview's leaders weighed this risk among the greater church body, I imagined they would preemptively plan meetings with the intention of clothing congregants with additional information, the kind that most of us would never think to reach for or inquire about. Instead, with the months of deliberation coming to a close, a single meeting had been planned, and it was scheduled to take place the weekend prior to the vote. The meeting was intended to share some details about the decision and to extend Fairview's congregants an opportunity to express outstanding questions; in turn, the leaders would be able to address them.

As the sole Q&A event approached, I confess being disappointed by the nature of the meeting as well as its late debut.

I also felt upset, frustrated with our leadership because the vote had drawn near while I felt no more prepared for it. However, I then felt guilty over my seemingly critical heart, believing I was somehow placing undue blame on Fairview's leaders. Though I was sad our elders did not more thoroughly equip us, I felt convicted, as if I were guilty of haphazardly assigning them responsibility for the personal unpreparedness on my part. Just because they had not handed us more information directly, I reasoned that I should not overreact emotionally, as if they were somehow seeking to withhold it.

In the final two weeks before the vote, I strived to let go of any outstanding grievances I held against Fairview's leadership. I specifically had to release the anger I felt toward the elders for placing the burden of gathering information upon individuals instead of forthrightly equipping them with it. Meanwhile, three questions circled my mind, ones that had been posed to us by the lead pastor when the elders' recommendation was shared with the congregants in the spring. *Was the amount of the proposed loan affordable? Was borrowing the money immoral?* And finally, *Did we trust our leadership?*

The three questions had not been included in the written material that the congregation received, nor were they posed in the video we watched. Instead, they were shared aloud with the church body in the early days that the proposal had been presented. My ability to recall such details would not normally prove so strong, but the questions remained in my mind throughout the summer months because at the time I heard them, they struck me as weird in more ways than one. Foremost, the questions did not draw us to consider God's wisdom and heart (i.e. the Bible) in the matter before us. Moreover, they sounded rudimentary and cold considering the fact that we faced such a serious decision. Finally, the questions echoed oddly in my soul because I knew they would never serve as the basis for deciding whether or not I bought something more personal, like a pair of shoes.

As the vote drew near, I tried to reconcile my feelings about the strange questions that had been posed in the spring, assuming I had heard them with greater weight than they had been intended to carry. Meanwhile, I found myself wishing that others did not readily recall the bizarre questions as distinctly as I had because I hoped congregants would not use them to determine which direction to cast their votes.

Trying to approach my decision objectively and wisely with the little time we had left before voting, another thought jumped to my mind which added to the concern I was already feeling. *I could not recall a single prayer session throughout the preceding months that had been committed to our decision.* The observation troubled me for several reasons, but one reason glared brighter than others.

By failing to readily and continually invite congregants to pray and seek God for his ultimate wisdom in our decision, I felt our leadership somehow maintained confidence that they had already obtained it. If that were true, I feared our elders were being presumptuous. And if congregants were to merely agree with the leadership's proposed direction, I believed the church body would be naive. The potential scenarios caused me to fear that we were about to approach God with pride and our vote with short-sightedness.

I observed the avenues we had taken as a church body to prepare for our vote, and every component that did or did not go into it. I felt increasingly insecure about the decision ahead and our church's ability to handle it wisely. Little time remained for us to assume a unified and wise stance as a congregation. Even so, Steve and I sought to capitalize on the opportunity we had left. The weekend before casting our ballots, we made plans to attend the Q&A event, the only meeting we knew about that had been created for the congregation to come together concerning our decision.

The meeting was scheduled to begin shortly after worship services ended on the Sunday prior to the congregational vote in an auxiliary section of the broadcast location. Steve and I decided to attend the Sunday morning worship service at the broadcast location since we would have to drive there for the meeting anyway. During the service, the lead pastor reminded the congregation about the impending vote the following weekend. I sat in the audience and listened in shock as he also told the congregation how he preferred them to vote.

Remaining stunned as we left the service, Steve and I grabbed a quick snack before we made our way to the Q&A meeting concerning the elders' proposal. Although the congregation was made up of nearly ten-thousand people, less than one-hundred attended, including many staff members required to be present because of their roles at Fairview. As the meeting commenced, a few congregants stood one-by-one and expressed questions or concerns. After each spoke, the leadership took time and responded to the given question or comment. When no more questions remained, the meeting drew to a close.

After a quiet drive home in the car, Steve and I instinctively embraced upon entering our home, and I immediately started sobbing. Regardless of the outcome of the forthcoming vote, I was upset over certain realities I had observed that morning. First, outstanding concerns and questions over the leaders' proposal were apparently few. Second, there was a miniscule number of people maintaining interest in hearing them as indicated by the congregational meeting's sparse attendance.

I was also troubled how the congregation was being guided, not necessarily forward, but in a particular direction. From the onset, the elders' proposal was worded in such a way that it clearly recommended the church body assume a certain course of action. As if the proposal's wording did not already lead the congregation to simply agree, the pastor had clearly indicated he wished they would, at least in the service Steve and I attended that morning. No matter which services had witnessed the pastor's spoken opinion, and how many parishioners had been actively listening, his words raised grave concern in my heart.

I believed the pastor had taken undue liberty in his role as a leader, if not by representing a leadership that specifically recommended a single course of action, then by explicitly asking that his respective church body concur with it. Moreover, my heart was deeply troubled as I strongly suspected that many congregants were likely to cast their vote based on our pastor's preference, without ever having examined the situation prayerfully and critically, despite being given many weeks to do so. Considering such an outcome to be very likely, I grew concerned, believing the congregation had bigger issues brewing than the imminent decision it faced.

The following weekend, church members voted at all campuses and all services. The proposal was approved by a sweeping majority. About 90% of Fairview Church's members affirmed the elders' recommendation. Inside the church that weekend, the vote seemed like a non-event. Because the idea of an expansion had been discussed for more than a year, the congregation appeared to merely affirm a previously drawn plan to solve a problem.

While the outcome of the vote seemed insignificant to some church members and a reason to celebrate for others, it wreaked havoc in my life and mind. I had thought the congregation might pass the proposal but was somehow wholly shocked when it did. The decision was much more significant than choosing to remodel a particular room like a kitchen or a bathroom. The decision we made surrounding the loan, and the cost attached to that decision, was mammoth. Had congregants done the math?

Conservatively, **interest** payments would cost $70,000/month (see p.128). Even for our large congregation, the amount felt unconscionable. Beyond its cost, I grieved knowing the facility would likely remain unoccupied most hours of most days. Deciding to spend so many millions on a structure seemed egregious, as if the church was more excited to honor their Christianity inside a building than exit the doors to practice it (James 1:27).

My love for Fairview Church was great, but my admiration and affection for it did not trump my personal convictions. The months preceding the congregational vote had been consequential to me. I had asked questions. I had prayed. I had sought God. Yet after the vote, I stood among the very small minority, and the implications were huge.

If others on our staff were opposed to the decision, I was not aware. Within our sizeable staff, I suddenly felt like I was on an island.

Apart from my husband, as far as I knew, I was the only one among friends and co-workers who voted not to affirm the proposal. And as firmly decided as the outcome had been, I was just as resolved in my stance against it. Meanwhile, I continually questioned, *How does God feel about this decision—and us as we made it?*

Internal mayhem ensued as questions bombarded my mind, especially regarding my church membership and employment. *What would happen next? When I showed up to work on Monday, would the leadership come to my office? Would I be asked to leave? Even if they didn't ask me to leave, could I imagine myself staying with the amount of unrest I was feeling about the church's decision?*

Though I felt devastated about the outcome of the vote, I did not talk about it with hardly anyone except Steve. On the Monday following the church's decision, I went to work and did my job as usual. Meanwhile, I kept praying about the result of the proposal as well as my reaction to it. In the days that followed, when I found myself troubled and alone at home or work, I tried to "talk myself down," attempting to convince myself that my convictions were wrong and that everyone else was right. However, my attempts to persuade myself that I was mistaken felt like I was lying to myself about the displeasure I felt God had with us.

As a result, one week after the congregational vote, because my soul felt so burdened and I genuinely believed we were making a monumental mistake before the living God, I decided to share my concerns with the person I deemed most appropriate to hear them. Since I easily get emotional and tongue tied when I try to talk about sizeable matters, I did not desire an in-person meeting of any kind. Instead, I put ink to paper and boiled my concerns and questions down to a few concise paragraphs. I addressed my one-page, typed letter to the lead pastor's home and dropped it in the mail.

Within a few days, the lead pastor stopped by my office unannounced and knocked on the door. The conversation lasted less than five minutes. He indicated the letter was received and appreciated, even read together with his wife. But by and large, my sentiments were not shared. I was sad but not surprised. The church had made its decision; now I was faced with my own.

Chapter 7

LEAVING

Stand up for what you believe in, even if you stand alone.

Suzy Kassem

A day or two after the lead pastor stopped by my office, the severity of the situation loomed over my head as I drove home from work and parked in the driveway. Sitting in the driver's seat, I dropped my head down and proceeded to have a colossal breakdown. Large amounts of tears and mucus came out of my eyes and nose respectively. Then, in the midst of my emotional turmoil, I experienced a moment of extreme clarity in reaching a certain conclusion: I simply could not stay.

To continue in my job meant remaining part of the congregation because that was a requirement to be a staff member. Even if it was not a requirement, I knew I could not continue working as part of a team while feeling so opposed to their direction. With my decision made, surrounded in the car with all my snotty tissues, I called my husband.

Answering while on his way home from work, my emotional state was a surprise to Steve, but my overall stance on the matter-at-hand was not. He and I had shared concerns about the elders' proposal and he, too, had voted against it. While I had enjoyed my job at Fairview for a few years, in more recent months, Steve had observed my increasing struggle. Feelings of tension had grown, and a heartfelt angst seemed to descend on me following the congregation's decision. On the phone, my thoughts spilled out to Steve afresh, then I flatly announced that I couldn't attend the church or work for it any longer.

My husband was caught off-guard. He and I were not the kind of people who quit one job before securing another. Steve was not angry or emotional. He heard the resolve in my voice and simply wanted to know "the plan" as he inquired about what I would do for future employment. I started sobbing again. I had no plan, and I told him that.

Steve listened with care as I told him I was compelled to do what felt right–resign. Even if it seemed unreasonable, the decision to leave my job with immediacy was the fitting one in my mind despite not having a new position waiting in the wings. In a matter of minutes, Steve understood and validated my state of unrest. We hung up, I walked inside, and in an evening of profound pain and clarity, I typed my resignation letter.

The next morning, I sat down at work and stared at my computer though I was wholly unable to concentrate on the contents in my inbox. When I saw my boss walk down the hallway, I awkwardly grabbed his attention and asked if we could sit down. He had barely taken a seat in my office when I extended a very shaky arm and handed him my resignation letter, simultaneously telling him about my decision.

My boss was caring and professional as always. He was clear that he did not want to see me go and asked me to stay, saying he would not speak of the matter to anyone for a day. I expressed gratitude for his kindness as well as his thoughtful offer, but as the day progressed, I did not retract my resignation. After a day came and went, a few other leaders learned of my leaving by word of mouth. One came to me and asked me to reconsider. He explained that the leadership of the church viewed differences of opinion among the staff as an asset. I thanked him for his kind approach but assured him I had made my decision, one that I was not inclined to change.

With my decision made, I did not feel like a bitter or angry person, nor did I grow into one during the days that followed. My resignation was also not some earth-shattering occurrence among the greater staff. Leaving employment from Fairview Church was infrequently seen as taboo; the church experienced a natural fluctuation of employees coming and going. Meanwhile, my manager continued to be kind to me as I worked the duration of my notice. We did not discuss my leaving often, but one day he reminded me that we cannot always control how specific problems are solved.

His words were not the first time I had heard them. I had come to him in the past when I observed some practice that seemed strange or inefficient. When I did, he explained that we might see a person using a hammer to complete a job that would be better accomplished with a screwdriver; however, it was less important that a specific matter be solved in a particular way than to have confidence that the ship as a whole sailed in the right direction. In the past, I believed the boat adhered to a reasonable course, but since I could no longer agree that it was, I maintained a sense of assurance in my decision to go.

Prior to my decision becoming more public, knowing that other staff members would hear about it, I initiated individual meetings with those I worked with most closely. To those few and anyone else who inquired, I offered a brief explanation as to why I resigned. I shared with each of them that my husband and I did not agree with the church's decision to affirm the elders' proposal, and the congregation's decision was significant enough for us to leave Fairview Church on account of it. My words were well received, and thankfully they were expressed without feelings of distress or through any tears.

After I explained my decision with one coworker who stopped by my office, she shared her own concerns over the church's decision. Though she confessed a measure of uncertainty whether the proposal was truly God's best for the church, she had voted in favor of it. Surprised that I would take such an extreme stance and leave my job, two different coworkers made me feel like my decision was a brave one. And still two other staff members spoke with me separately about my departure, one on the phone and another on a picnic bench. Each listened while insinuating at the end of our conversation that they were personally in favor of Fairview's direction.

In addition to the handful of one-on-one conversations that I shared with staff members, during the next monthly staff meeting, my name was presented among a short list of individuals exiting their employment from the church. Most biographies for departing staff members usually included a reason for the person's departure, explanations like "becoming a mom" or "planting a church." My exit biography offered no real reason for my going; it simply stated that I was leaving my job and looking forward to whatever God had in store for me. Over the following weeks, my season on staff drew quietly to a close. My transition and ultimate departure lasted a few months, and except working well beyond a two-week notice, my exit from employment was otherwise quite normal. On the determined day, I turned over my keys and walked out the door.

I left Fairview with a clean conscience about my decision and without animosity, resentment, bitterness or anger. Such emotions had not driven my decision to leave, nor did they take residence in my heart upon my departure. In the leaving process, I was not tempted to create a scene, nor was one playing out in my mind. I was sad about losing a church and my job there, but more than mourning those things, I was grieved over the congregation's decision.

My walk with the Lord was not without effect on account of my season at Fairview, and the church's positive influence in my life was one reason the congregation's decision was difficult to watch. In my mind, the church had chosen a path that undermined God's glory. Their direction saddened me because the church often appeared to magnify the Lord's greatness during my seven years as an attendee, including the two-and-a-half years I worked among its staff. Fairview's trajectory now appeared contrary to the direction it most consistently seemed to go, one complementary to God's heart and for the greater good.

As part of the congregation, I had felt genuinely caught up in God's activity around New Haven. In choosing to leave the church, I felt sad knowing that the byproducts I was walking away from were not just polished programs and organized outreach efforts. Parishioners at Fairview regularly encountered God in personal ways, well beyond the church's walls. In turn, personal testimonies were sometimes captured on video and played during worship services, encouraging the church body at large.

Whenever I watched a video testimonial during a service, I felt as if God was especially near. The sense of closeness caused me to imagine that when he peered down on New Haven, God smiled at us. And just as I believed he delighted in Fairview, so did I. Facing such a big transition in my life, I trusted God for what was ahead, but also acknowledged the magnitude of what I was leaving behind.

Walking away from the megachurch, I pondered what church might be next in my journey and wondered what congregation could ascend the sizeable wake that Fairview left on me and my life. Meanwhile, I ran smack into my cynical side as I also questioned where else I would find parishioners that were not pew warmers.

Immediately recognizing my poor attitude, I cut myself some slack. Gaining affinity for a new church would understandably take time. I had attended Fairview for several years and with every song we had sung, sermon we had heard, and God-story we had witnessed, I had truly become partial to Fairview Church. I believed God understood my heart and that he held special regard for the church too because, frankly, Fairview was the best.

Chapter 8

PRIDE

A proud man is always looking down on things and people; and, of course, as long as you are looking down, you cannot see something that is above you.

CS Lewis

Let me pause for a moment. At the time I attended and worked for Fairview Church, to the best of my knowledge, I did not do so in an overtly proud manner. I did not go around telling everyone that I thought I attended the best church in New Haven. If asked, I merely talked about Fairview Church with sincere affection as is usual among most Christian, church-going people. So, the pride I maintained as a church member and that I can plainly see now was inconspicuous to me then. Simply speaking, I wanted to be a good Christian and believed my church of choice was at least partially indicative of that resolve.

As a Christ follower, I was determined to live out my Christian faith to the greatest extent possible. I knew Jesus was my Savior, and because of my affection and commitment to Christ, I wanted to learn about him and love him to my utmost ability. In seeking to love Jesus well, I wanted to be on the best possible path to grow in God. And I believed I was becoming the best Christian that I could be, at least in part because I thought I attended the best church in our city–which is also why I had a Fairview Church bumper sticker on my car.

Sporting the sticker on my car did not solely speak to my affection for the church; it also served as an invitation to others.

My love for the church naturally resulted in a desire for new people to become a part of our congregation. I felt certain that if other drivers across the city saw the bumper sticker on my car and on the cars of other Fairview Church members, they would eventually come to recognize our church's name. If they knew the name of Fairview Church and grew curious enough to visit, they may ultimately join the congregation.

I was not wrong to care deeply about my particular local church, and I was not incorrect in wanting others to join a church body that sincerely loved God. However, I was in error by esteeming a church's name, pastor and reputation more than the people inside it. I had not realized it when Fairview's name was riding on my bumper, but after leaving the church, I more clearly understood why I had been pleased to place the magnet on my car. My desire to display the church's symbol was not rooted in deep love for its members, but the satisfaction I felt through my association with the church because it was prestigious.

While a member at Fairview Church, I knew some members to some extent, but the relationships I experienced within the congregation were not the reason I esteemed the church in some special way. In fact, I rarely initiated consistent and caring acts towards church members, and I knew few members well enough that I was ever so inclined. However, I did feel proud to associate with the church because of its renowned pastor, talented musicians, professional sounding play lists, and parishioners who maintained a reputation for being eager to engage the community. Therefore, more than anything, I maintained a heart-felt allegiance for "the body," that is, the church's name and my affiliation with it.

I did not recognize it at the time but, according to my perception of Fairview Church and my most common interactions with it, the church was less a group of people that I loved and more an enterprise I esteemed. When I saw my church–Fairview Church–I saw it as the "best" church within our large and sprawling metropolis. And I did not just see it as the best church for me; I saw it as the church that many others were missing out on because they were at "that other church."

- They wore suits and dressed up, placing value on physical appearance before God. We welcomed jeans, and projected the message: "Come as you are."

- They sang from individual hymnals. We sang from a shared screen.

- They had printed bulletins. We were more earth-conscious.

- They had a greeter or two at the door. We had a greeter team (with greeters in the parking lot, at the front door, and positioned at a welcome table). And we gave you a gift.

- They held Sunday School classes in church buildings. We had small groups in homes mid-week and sought to "do-life together."

- They had worship services for one hour. We met for longer because we needed more time for teaching and singing. We were not just doing a duty; we loved being at services even if it took a little extra time.

- They had a pastor who spoke from the Bible but did not consistently captivate listeners or evoke critical thought. We had a pastor who engaged our minds and challenged our ways, as well as those listening on-line, including those around the globe.

- They had less God-sightings, I imagined. We had life-change happening in the lives of our congregation and had video testimonials as part of our services to tell about it.

- They had services on Sunday, as that was tradition. We were open-minded and willing to adjust to new worship schedules, even adding multiple Saturday services. Our adaptability was a byproduct of our willingness to keep building costs down while creating open seats for new people to know Jesus.

- They sustained older church buildings with stained glass and static attendance. We met in non-traditional buildings that weren't fancy while also giving to one-fund campaigns so that more could be reached with the gospel of Jesus Christ.

- They had an older population and esteemed Christian tradition in services. We touched on tradition but also embraced a Christian expression that was relevant for today's generation.

- Their church bodies were growing some or staying stagnant in number. We were drawing new Christians, people were being baptized en masse, and we were regularly identified in Christian publications as one of the fastest growing churches in the nation.

After leaving the church, I had time and space to recognize my subconscious and prevailing thoughts. As a result, I saw that I was super judgmental and equally blind. I criticized how other church bodies celebrated their Christianity in the hours they gathered; in turn, I looked down on those choosing to assemble as part of them.

Compared to Fairview, I saw other local churches and their congregants as inferior in their faith. My pride and sin ran so deep, and the comparison was so subconscious, I did not even realize I was doing it. As a result, I became what I had always detested. Holding such pride for Fairview Church, I came to embody the sinful behavior that I had hated and been subject to even in my youth.

Through childhood and into adulthood, I met others who held allegiance to their church. Often, their devotion extended deep into the denomination in which their church was a part. As a child raised in church, denominations were of no great consequence to me. What did bother me was when people acted as if their particular Christian denomination was the true church, the one church, the right church, or the only real church. I heard or perceived many such notions throughout my life, and the impressions always left me confused or offended.

In middle school, I had a friend sleep-over at my home on Saturday, and the next morning she had to go home in order to go to church even though my family was church-going. As I waved goodbye, I wondered, *Was my family's church not good enough?* In my teen years, I went to church with a friend and accidentally partook of the Lord's Supper. I say it was accidental because I didn't know I was not allowed. Though part of God's family, I learned afterward that I had not been welcome at that communion table.

The confusion continued into Christian adulthood. Upon college graduation, I observed some peers marry outside of their denomination and noticed the decision was not inconsequential to certain family members on one side or the other. I then experienced some of the same disharmony as I dated different people; a given boyfriend would have his church, and I would have mine. In one relationship, I did a church "circuit" the few months we dated. Sunday mornings, I often attended my boyfriend's church for the early service then went to my own church for the late service. I felt glad about visiting the church that meant so much to my boyfriend, despite feeling sad that he never stepped foot in mine.

At other times in adulthood, I wrestled as a hostess in trying to love and respect Christian guests in my home. If visitors stayed for the weekend, I would attend Fairview Church on Saturday and then join my out-of-town guests at their preferred church service or denomination on Sunday. Considering I loved my guests and we all loved Jesus, I could not deny how awkward and un-sanctimonious it felt.

These ever-surfacing issues about denominational and church preferences caused ongoing confusion and discomfort. For this reason, I disliked interactions with others when they insinuated that one denomination or church had superiority over others. Whenever I was subjected to it, I detested it. Yet because of the pride I developed for Fairview Church, I inadvertently came to embody it.

Regarding Fairview, I did not see the church's denomination as superior, but I adopted the same underlying pride about how great Fairview Church was within the specific city of New Haven. I judged our congregation as living more consequentially Christian than other local congregations, so I deemed us better. I had despised notions rooted in denominational arrogance, but the pride I held for my personal congregation was no better. It just took me leaving to see it.

I left Fairview, resolved to extricate myself from sins I

believed the church was committing. Little did I know that in leaving, I would run head-first into a host of my own. The haughtiness I had about Fairview Church was only the first place God would put his finger. Though it had been unplanned, stepping away from Fairview helped me gain clarity in my relationship to it as well as other churches I had attended throughout my years as a Christian. Suddenly, standing apart from all congregations, I discovered a more objective perspective concerning them. God showed me that I was prone to recognize corporate sins quicker than personal ones. In turn, he flipped my lens of observation 180 degrees, and the sorrow I felt over Fairview quickly turned into sadness over self. His new business with me felt much like a personal undoing. In the midst of it, mindsets I long-held as true and right, both on the surface and deep in the subconscious, were challenged.

◆◆◆

In the preceding pages, I have shared my story as if a good friend of mine had passed through town, one I hadn't seen or spoken to in some time. I described my situation in large part as if that old confidant had settled across the couch and asked, "How is it that you are currently unemployed?" In the remaining chapters, I have sought to preserve the same candor; however, my earnest thoughts are presented in an altogether different manner.

During the months following my departure from Fairview, my life morphed from the familiar to the unscripted. My husband and I visited a host of churches and frequented a few of them. Normal routines changed quite a bit and so did several viewpoints that I had maintained about my Christian life. Perspectives and experiences that had been concrete became fluid, topics on the table for examination with God. Each area the Lord addressed became complementary to a greater and ongoing lesson, one bearing increased closeness with him and wider respect for his greater Church.

The remaining pages have been written in alternate fashion and do not tie seamlessly together in story form. Instead, I have laid out a handful of stand-alone thoughts, ones I would share with the same old friend if she darkened my door a year following my resignation and asked, "How have you changed since I saw you last?"

Part II

CHANGE

(true statements that were not always true)

Chapter 9

GOOD DEEDS

There are two kinds of people, those who do the work and those who take the credit. Try to be in the first group; there is less competition there.

Indira Gandhi

I do not blame the church for my inactivity in doing good.

As a Christian, I have always had an inherent desire to get out and do good in my little corner of the world, but I have felt frustrated by this inclination when I haven't known suitable channels in which to act on it. For most of my Christian walk, I believed that providing congregants with places to serve was the responsibility of each local church. So when I attended any given church and found its community service opportunities sparse, I often placed blame on the church.

Fairview Church provided several opportunities to become a volunteer, but at the time I attended, they were primarily ways that supported weekend worship services like greeting, seating, prayer teams, or volunteering with children. The church also held some sizeable events for congregants to serve outside its doors on an annual basis, but identifying consistent and ongoing opportunities to volunteer outside of the congregation proved difficult.

Once, I remember being interested in a mentorship program that was structured, established, and provided a chance to serve regularly over the course of many months. At the time, it was one of the few formal opportunities to serve within the community year-round. I was excited and went to the training session one weekend which lasted a handful of hours. However, I learned that the program's structure required each mentor to meet with their assigned mentee on a day within the school week, specifically during a time in the middle of the afternoon. As I started pursuing the steps to become a mentor, it perplexed me how "normal" people with full-time jobs could feasibly serve as one. In turn, I never invested time volunteering in the program apart from the hours to learn about it one Saturday morning.

Seeing few other options to serve consistently in a capacity beyond the church's walls, I felt stymied and frustrated. I was perplexed that the church did not create more ways for congregants to get involved in the community. Partnerships between non-profit organizations in the city and Fairview Church seemed almost non-existent, and I couldn't understand why.

Largely because of its great size, Fairview Church had a large pool of Christian people inherently inclined to do good. However, its leaders appeared to be hampering volunteerism because they were not providing a vast number of avenues for congregants to give of their resources and time. Though able, church leaders were not deliberately and wholeheartedly establishing conduits to send congregants into the city as volunteers, encouraging them to develop relationships in the community in varying capacities and on a more regular basis throughout the year.

As a Christ-follower desirous of living out my Christianity by helping to meet the practical needs of others, I believed Fairview Church maintained an inherent duty to be the hub of opportunity. I felt that most organizations meeting various needs in our community should be connected to the church in some capacity. The partnerships between such organizations and Fairview Church would create an easy on-ramp for me and potentially thousands of other Christians within our congregation to serve and engage the community. Because the avenues to serve were few, I viewed the church as failing the members of the body as well as indirectly neglecting the individuals that the congregation would otherwise be serving.

As a result, blame and frustration towards the church simmered in my subconscious. Instead of wanting to engage in acts of service as I progressed in my Christian walk, in some regards, I became increasingly apathetic. Because I regularly felt pigeonholed in the options available to offer my time and talents, I became disenchanted and cynical when considering volunteerism, even though the thought of it previously excited me. The disinterest that grew in me in regards to serving, combined with my unwillingness to serve in ways that I knew about but did not especially enjoy, felt like the church's fault.

My frustration concerning service opportunities did not wane during my time at Fairview Church. Even so, my love for weekend services usually silenced my grumblings about how I felt the church at large was defunct in volunteerism and how much I believed Fairview's leaders were responsible. Most of the time, I was not cognizant of the expectations that I was placing on the church's leadership, thinking they should provide opportunities for me and other congregants to serve. On the occasions my feelings flared and I was aware, I never considered that my expectations could be wrong.

Only after finding myself in a season without a church home did I realize how deeply I had blamed Fairview Church for failing to create what I deemed to be suitable opportunities to live my Christian life more practically. The season in solitude with God and without a new church home revealed how deeply I felt the church had somehow wronged me, as well as the entire church body, in failing to provide more chances for us to demonstrate our faith in Christ to those outside the church's walls.

As I reflected, I saw that I also largely expected Fairview Church to create service opportunities that were unique to my interests as well as personally appealing. While I think some of my expectations may have been inherent, I also came to believe that they were in-part the result of certain sermons I had heard throughout my years as a Christian. As a church-goer at various congregations, I was encouraged on more than one occasion to invest time identifying my spiritual gifts. At the close of such a sermon, a church leader would often direct congregants to resources to aid the process, like surveys, inventories, or separate classes on spiritual gifting. But while churches seemed to affirm that unique talents existed within a congregation, they did not appear to place equal energy in fostering opportunities for congregants to thrive in them. The lack of places to "plug-in" and to flourish in a specific form of servitude left me wanting, but it also left me feeling strangely wounded and sometimes angry.

As a member of various church bodies, I surveyed the choices I had to volunteer and naturally looked for ones that were in harmony with my personality. Given the choice to assist with an event, I would clean instead of cook. I would stuff backpacks before I would choose to engage school officials and deliver them. Similarly, I would prefer to donate items to the nursery than to be found in it on a Sunday morning. While I was not wrong to prefer one job over another, my degree of disappointment in having limited options to serve indicated that, to some degree, I had come to glamorize servitude.

By wanting the church to create opportunities for me to volunteer that I deemed fitting to my personality, I was inadvertently expecting the church to help me experience a greater sense of fulfillment in my life, particularly as a unique child of God's. While I wanted to do good and help others, I cannot deny that I also wanted to feel a measure of personal joy and satisfaction in the process. Just as church leaders desired me to know my gifts, I wanted the leaders to help me operate purposefully and well in them.

Upon leaving the church and becoming aware of my grievances and how much I felt the church had fallen short in helping me to thrive in my God-given capacity, I first felt inclined to forgive the church's offense. Second, I felt led to consider whether the transgressions against me were true or perceived. Answering the latter helped steer me into a more appropriate action concerning the church and my attitude toward it: repentance.

I still maintain a desire to do good, including specific acts that are of particular interest to me, and I do not think these desires are ignoble. However, I no longer expect the local church to function as a "Grand Central Station" in regards to service opportunities, because my belief that it should have operated that way was logical but it was not biblical. I came to understand that while God called his children to employ their talents for the good of others (1Peter 4:10), church bodies and their leaders were never made responsible for facilitating their backdrop.

◆◆◆

I do not look at my local church as a good-deed umbrella policy.

After becoming a Christian and graduating from college, I placed a lot of my focus on good works. Jesus said we should do them (James 2:14-26), and as I grew in my faith, I observed that helping others is a natural desire for most Christians. Though often insecure in how many good deeds I was or wasn't doing, I found that I felt most assured in this particular area of my life during the years that I attended Fairview Church.

Despite knowing that a Christian quota of good works does not exist and that I can do nothing to earn my way to heaven, I confess having a recurring, subconscious battle concerning what I am doing or not doing in response to the immeasurable love God has shown me through Christ. I seem to automatically contemplate my life regularly, wondering how I am specifically living for God in my actions and choices in light of what he has already done and continues to do for me.

My inner musings often play on a reel, *What are you doing to show God that you love Him this week? Are you being lazy? Are you leveraging what He's given you in a way that brings him glory? Are you dedicating your time, talents, and personal belongings to Him and are you using them for His purposes? Are your comfortable? If you are, does that mean you're idle, not living life how God has prescribed? God, do you find my everyday life pleasing, particularly how I am investing the time, money and talents you have given me?*

As far as acts of doing good, I have always wanted to know that I am engaged in the right amount–whatever that measure is. I have longed for some sense of assurance, to know that I was doing enough deliberate activities, ones eternally meaningful and markedly good. If I hit that mark, then my sense of questioning would be replaced by a feeling of confidence—not a greater confidence concerning salvation—but in knowing that I was not wasting my days living inconsequentially as a Christian.

I started to feel more secure in my measure of doing good, largely when I attended Fairview Church. The church had been established for many years, and by the time I became a member, it already held a reputation for being loving towards those outside of it. When I saw the good the megachurch was accomplishing through their periodic and annual service projects, I naturally assigned myself personal Christian credit. In my mind, I was reflecting Jesus more brightly because of the shiny fruit with which I identified. I took the impressive city-wide impact of our congregation and associated myself with its benevolent acts in a personal way.

I internalized the church's servitude, believing the host of good deeds were at least partially my accomplishments because I was one representative of the whole. Doing so gave me a sense of personal assurance that I was attending a solid church as well as living my life as a legitimate Christian. I did not realize it at the time, but my church became my personal do-good Christian crutch. In being associated with a church known by many for its service within the city, I felt greater peace of mind about the act of serving despite how often I actually engaged in it. The display of good works done by the church body somehow provided me with increased subconscious assurance regarding my own benevolence, simply being one of its members.

In essence, Fairview's volunteerism acted as an umbrella of good deeds in case I were stagnant in my own for a week, a month, or more. It was a contract that I had silently concocted as part of my personal Christianity, and it was one deeply hidden in my mind and heart. And though I had been blind to it, the silent-contract served me well because, whether inside the church or outside of it, I often struggled with a lack of desire to volunteer. No matter the span of my lethargy or absence in greeting, seating or accompanying the prayer team, I was able to calm my conscience on account of the acts done by my congregation. Though I never expected my personal good works or those of the church to solidify my salvation, the church members' kind deeds did make me feel better when I personally felt sad or convicted concerning a lack of my own.

Finding myself in a season alone with God and without a church home, I was left naked in a sense. I was no longer able to attribute the good deeds of other people or a church body to myself. Instead, I had the opportunity to recognize I had been citing corporate good deeds to my flawed Christian conscience in the first place. I also had time and space to better understand why the desire to "do good" was never far from my mind.

Sojourning in solitude, I realized that I had aspired to do good works in hopes of pleasing God. My good desire was actually bad, because it revealed I was attempting to earn what Jesus already paid for—my perfect standing with God. In striving to earn God's pleasure, I failed to accept I already had it. Recognizing my wrong thinking, I learned to rest in what Christ had done. In turn, my relationship with God became stronger, and the healthier bond reframed the experiences I aspired to or encountered each day.

Before my season of self-reflection, I felt compelled that as a Christian I should go out and "do ministry." I mostly saw doing ministry as separate from normal life because going to work and shopping for groceries didn't constitute "Christian" activities in my mind. Therefore, I felt inclined to look for opportunities to do things that more overtly reflected the kindness of Christ towards others. In many ways, I put my focus on that resolve (regardless if I was actually doing it) more than I lived to be a ministering person, demonstrating kindness, patience and compassion–at work, in the car, or at the grocery store.

Embracing my right-standing with God, I thought about benevolent tasks I "should be" doing less often. Rather, I started to focus on my ongoing posture of heart. In expending energy to daydream about benevolence (or feeling guilt over my failure to carry it out), to some extent, I had actually robbed that resource from real people in my life. Realizing this, I learned to place less focus on finding a "Christian" opportunity in front of me, resolving to be an effective Christ-follower by giving my full attention to the moment, person, interaction, or activity directly in front of me.

Chapter 10

VISION & VALIDATION

Accepting the invitation to show up in life is about moving from the bleachers to the field. It's moving from developing opinions to developing options. It's about having things matter to us enough that we stop just thinking about those things and actually do something about them.

Bob Goff

I do not inherently look to others for permission.

In any church, someone in each local body is making decisions about what can or cannot be done as far as congregational ministries, projects and pursuits. I have historically respected this process of decision making within churches because it seems to result in peace and order. Yet I confess the authority of decision makers has sometimes frustrated me because of its byproduct: unrealized potential.

In other words, upholding the authority of a few can result in limiting effects for those yielding to that authority. Concerning projects, ministries and initiatives, I have observed how church leaders appear to hold a special stamp of approval, either allowing congregants to formulate new endeavors or gently patting them on the back for their desire.

Not long after I began my employment at Fairview Church, I heard a coworker talk about how he had just received a call from a very excited woman. She called the church because she had discovered a passion for a particular local organization, and she felt that everyone in the congregation should know about the opportunities to serve there. The staff member appreciated her enthusiasm but gently explained that advertising the organization and service opportunity before the congregation was not plausible.

Hearing him talk about the account left an impression on me. As a fellow congregant desirous of doing good, I understood the woman's heart. I respected her inclination to petition those within the church, to create an open door for more congregants to practice benevolence. But as a staff member, I also accepted the fact that time restrictions and other parameters prevented her particular service opportunity and many other potential announcements to be advertised each week.

Since then, I have wondered about the woman and the ministry in which she was excited because I, too, have been captivated by specific do-good opportunities and on occasion have dreamed about starting new ones. Similarly, I have wanted a chance to share about them, particularly before church bodies, in anticipation of others showing interest in joining me; but I have also been faced with what the woman likely felt: a sense of sadness on account of being inadvertently prevented.

In the months leading up to my resignation and in the months that followed, I came to better understand that a host of invisible walls surround most congregations. In some cases, the partition can stand between a congregant and the rest of his or her own congregation, like the woman excited for the church to endorse her cause. Other times, invisible walls can keep fellow Christians who are outside a given congregation from being able to share about new or existing initiatives with those who are gathered inside.

Around the time I left my job and church home, I learned about a local young woman who had created a website where potential volunteers and donors could explore opportunities to satisfy needs within New Haven. Through her site, a host of wants within the community could be met. For example, a Good Samaritan could visit the site, note that toiletries were needed at a local women's shelter, and drop-off a bag of unused hotel soaps.

The website was a tool to be used by those living in New

Haven, and it was one that interested me because I was a part of a small group of individuals seeking to create a similar online resource. My team members and I wanted to learn from the website's creator, so I reached out to her through her site and inquired about an opportunity to speak with her. I was excited to receive her reply while confirming through her response that she was also a Christian.

Kara, the creator of the website, was willing to speak with me, and not much later, we were able to connect on the phone. I inquired about a handful of things, and as we wrapped up our time, one of my last questions was, "How have you advertised your website to church leaders, and how has it been received?" She responded, "That's been the most frustrating part [of creating the site]." She went on to explain how she had met with multiple local church leaders to share about the website, but the experiences ultimately left her wanting.

When Kara met with church leaders in person, they seemed supportive. But after several meetings at different churches, she experienced no real follow-through. Kara had shared with pastors and church leaders who affirmed her efforts and website while she was sitting with them, but to her knowledge, they never actively directed their congregants to the site. As she answered my question, she shared that she had little sense that any person of prominence who had met with her was actively encouraging their respective local body to engage it, to discover ways of meeting various needs within the community through it.

I observed the frustration she conveyed, and just hearing the disappointment in her voice led me to feel a measure of it myself. Kara's experience helped me to see how often church leaders operated like gatekeepers, "official" people that offered a stamp of approval for the ideas of others, even ideas birthed outside the domain of their respective churches. For instance, Kara had created something innovative through her own initiative, but her desire to see it fully thrive drove her directly to an array of church doors as she asked church leaders to catalyze her efforts.

Listening to her story, I understood Kara's desire to seek

help from church leaders. I also instinctively understood how invaluable their endorsement could be. Kara's situation showed me how the advocacy of church leaders could impact whether a ministry or project might be primed, where Christians at large could learn about it and aid its success. Even the influence of social media seemed less effective than a church leader's plug, at least from my observation. First, a proponent of a given nonprofit may not necessarily be on any social media platforms. Or, the advocate could "tweet" and "post" about a service opportunity while the individuals most interested in listening might remain missing from their audience.

On the other hand, I observed how each local church naturally maintained a target audience in regards to people inclined to do good. In turn, church leaders seemed to hold a tremendous amount of potential in their ability to pass along information regarding specific chances to be charitable; however, they could also elect not to share about such opportunities with their congregations. I realized that Kara and other Christian pioneers like her could omit the involvement of local churches instead of asking their respective leaders for help, but I also acknowledged that doing so was inherently unnatural.

Kara's situation touched me in a personal way and showed me how much I was inclined to relate to the local church as if I was in a parent-child relationship with it. Though seemingly benign, relating to the church that way caused me to have a less than healthy relationship with it. For instance, as a church member for most of my life, I rarely considered my own creativity in cultivating new outlets in living the Christian life in the world around me. Instead, I defaulted to exploring only the existing ministries within a given church. And more recently, if I had a new ministry idea and approached the church concerning it, I felt like I was seeking permission to play outside the fenced-in yard.

If what I envisioned doing for and with God was not ultimately encouraged and endorsed by church leadership, I felt stymied. Like Kara experienced, the ability to pursue visions with any measure of success seemed to hinge on at least one church—likely the one I was a part—advocating my efforts. Not having the church's endorsement caused me to feel as if I were not allowed to attempt something new or that I was doomed to certain failure if I tried. Speaking with Kara also led me to see how I was among other Christians who naturally gravitated to churches for approval or at least advocacy, a phenomenon I experienced afresh in the months following my conversation with her.

Prior to leaving Fairview, I encountered an absurd but ongoing inclination to establish a craft fair, one that would specifically benefit the community of North Haven. The notion was an odd one, especially coming from a person unlikely to create anything worthy of cash. But because the unction was unrelenting, I shared my idea with a few friends. Meanwhile, I started brainstorming ways that I could carry it out and made a list of elements required to bring it to fruition. I would need a location for the event, so I started considering every possible place that might be a suitable space for free. Meanwhile, I needed vendors for the event, crafters who would not mind sharing their proceeds with a worthwhile cause. Instinctively, I believed the broadest pool of charitable people would be found sitting in church sanctuaries on the weekends.

Thinking Christian crafters would be most inclined to participate, I baked a bunch of chocolate chip cookies and drove them to about a half-dozen churches. Walking into each church, I handed a package of cookies to the first person to greet me and included a note to the church staff. In the card, I invited their congregants to the craft fair and asked them to consider taking part in the event as a vendor. I explained that the craft show was not sponsored by any particular congregation, but that several churches in the area were invited to participate together. I also included my email address and the dates and times of an informational meeting. In addition to the churches I visited, I looked up a few nearby congregations on-line. I gathered contact information for their staff members and emailed them the same invitation.

Of the handful of church offices that I visited and emailed, I never heard back from a single staff member. Though I am not sure how many church leaders may or may not have advertised the event to their greater church body, to my knowledge, only two crafters came from the congregations I specifically invited. The manner in which the two crafters learned about the event may have been through their church, or they may have learned about the craft fair the same way that the rest of the participants did–by word of mouth, by my poised but pointed invitations through Etsy, or by way of a public website that specifically advertised craft fairs.

In the end, a few close friends and twenty-two creative souls helped pull off New Haven's first ever Community Craft Fair. Ultimately, the event was not technically a money-making one; my husband and I paid for the venue out-of-pocket, but a kind church did allow us to use the space at a discount. Still, the experience was well worth the efforts and cost in my mind.

The crafters had fun and offered solid feedback through a survey we sent after the event. A local ministry was gifted several hundred dollars, a portion of the proceeds of all that was sold. I maintained a sense of personal satisfaction because I felt that I had been obedient to the Lord and his promptings by orchestrating the event. And I learned that while I had instinctively counted on churches to champion my cause and aid its success, they were not essential in making an endeavor dedicated to God both possible and worthwhile.

As a result of Kara's experience in addition to my own, these days I would say I look at the local church like a school in which I am a student. The new way I relate to the local church has led my relationship with it to be healthier. The church facilitates my learning as a follower of God, but if I am not permitted to do certain Christian-minded "experiments" that stir my heart and soul inside their walls or with their assistance, I know I can simply step outside.

Now if I am inspired with a vision or idea, I am less inclined to work towards it while expecting a local church to determine its launch or facilitate its success. Instead, I am better prepared to move prayerfully forward while employing social platforms and the efforts of wanting individuals. In the absence of a church home, I developed a greater desire for me and all Christians to not stop exploring creative ministry ideas or pursuits, regardless of a church's endorsement. Moreover, I believe more than ever that church leaders do not have the final say about God's vision and direction in the lives of his children, and I should not think and act as if they do.

Simply speaking, I believe that a church's lack of endorsement or affirmation of a vision does not necessarily imply that God is not the author of it. I maintain that God is able to bring each vision to his desired end, but as I continue to walk with the Lord, I am more persuaded than ever to not stop short of that end. Meanwhile, if a local church is willing to catalyze my efforts, I will see that as a blessed provision. On the other hand, if they are not willing to support my endeavor, I will resist perceiving their inactivity as an obstacle.

In the past, when I attended various churches, I looked at their established ministries and considered my options. More recently, I have learned to exercise new freedom in looking beyond existing ministries, because I know that God may prompt me to do something apart from them. I have also stopped looking to church leaders for their validation. Instead, I recognize my own ability to hear God's voice and follow his promptings.

Boiled down, I believe the crux of the matter is this: God's presence or absence in a vision or project is not determined by a church because churches are excellent but at times errant. As a result, a church may fail to champion me in a Lord-led cause while sustaining another man's vision that is not God's, one that continually utilizes the congregation's time, energy and resources. In seeking to nurture a vision, I recognize that it is less important for a church to partner with me than for me to stay partnered with the God who I believed to have authored it.

My growing faith persuades me that godly ideas can take root outside those accepted and affirmed within a church's walls. Carried to fruition, I also believe their ripple effects may be felt far beyond the sphere of any congregation. Moreover, visions birthed and fostered beyond the jurisdiction of a formal church can be especially meaningful and momentous. First, the man who partners with God in such a personal way grows spiritually, regardless of what his outward efforts produce. Second, the glory that God receives through such endeavors does not have to compete with the praise that is sometimes given to a church.

Chapter 11

SMALL GROUPS

A rat in a maze is free to go anywhere, as long as it stays inside the maze.

Margaret Atwood

I do not believe small groups are necessary.

As a member of the megachurch, I was grateful for the ways church leaders desired to care for me. When the church connected me to a small group, I felt they were loving me well, wanting me to grow through fellowship and closeness with other Christians. Personally, I so deeply affirmed the concept of small groups (or community groups, life groups, growth groups, cell groups, etc.), that I am not sure I would have attended a church without them.

I believed participation in a small group was significant because the weekly gatherings provided consistency in my life and relationships. Assembling with others, I liked knowing I was not living the Christian life alone. Moreover, church leaders highly encouraged congregants to join a small group. Approximately a dozen people made up the size of most groups, and participating in them helped me get to know a handful of individuals in our huge congregation more personally.

In my experience, small groups were not without frustrations. Some group members had personalities that were difficult for me to understand, and sometimes, my patience was tried when one or two people talked far more than others. Still, I could not imagine foregoing a small group. Attending weekend church services was enriching and enjoyable, but in our large sanctuary, I hardly ever knew the parishioners sitting next to me. On the other hand, my small group created a much more personal atmosphere. We met weekly, discussed the Bible, talked about life, and sometimes shared a meal.

The church's small group ministry was intricate and felt like a gift. The leadership had the privilege of knowing the big picture. Of the thousands of congregants in the megachurch, they maintained everyone's zip codes and street addresses. Apart from a small group directory, trying to find other congregants that lived near me in order to cultivate relationships would likely prove difficult. The church had many campuses, but even at one location, members might drive substantial distances from opposite directions. Accessing a list of small group locations and their designated meeting days and times was a welcomed tool, and it helped me successfully connect with others by proximity and availability.

I was rarely not in a small group, and I was a part of a few small groups for a decent duration of approximately two years. During my years in a small group, I sought to be a committed member, so I changed groups infrequently. I stopped attending one group when I became a foster parent, feeling as though I did not have the bandwidth to continue while juggling new responsibilities. I stopped attending another because our leader moved out-of-state and personal circumstances changed for other members, so the group essentially dissolved.

The people in my small groups were kind. We shared a bit about our personal struggles, prayed for one another, and at times helped one another with things like yard sales, child care, or moving. Still, I often felt like I was left wanting something more. I could not reconcile my outstanding desire for *more* because as a small group, we met faithfully, studied Bible passages, discussed the corresponding sermon and answered thought-provoking questions that were relevant to God's Word and our lives.

Despite these wonderful things, I wondered if I was the only one who had unsettled feelings at times, like our interactions were cautiously courteous and not altogether candid. Though we did not force one another to engage or share, sometimes I felt like our conversation was somewhat manufactured. We seemed to seek an air of intimacy, but I felt as if we were largely going through set motions. We prayed, studied and shared with one another, but I could not deny that real relationships felt elusive. By and large, I did not feel especially close with those in my group though we were obviously devoted, meeting nearly every week. My experience felt ironic because I genuinely desired transparency and intimacy in relationships, but that kind of depth was difficult to cultivate with those in my group.

Resigning from my job and leaving Fairview was unexpected, but so was the subsequent loss of my formal tie to a small group. Leaving the church meant that I would not maintain my participation in a small group through it. Not having a small group left me feeling uneasy because for several years of my Christian walk, I had placed as much emphasis on my participation in a small group as I did my weekly worship attendance. Though unwanted, the absence of a small group and church home provided an opportunity to look at my small group experiences more objectively.

First, I realized that my small groups routinely embraced a hiatus during the summer months. The decision was not uncommon and was also culturally accepted because groups often patterned their schedules according to the traditional school year. Additionally, people's lives often grew especially busy during summer months. As a result, small group meetings seemed to fall to the back burner from late May through the first week of September.

Before we stopped meeting, leaders encouraged group members to use the weeks ahead to connect more casually with one another in lieu of our traditional gatherings. Usually, we were told the group would meet once or twice during the hiatus for a meal, recreation and fun. Meanwhile, the leaders and members assumed that the relationships would survive and we would reconvene in the fall. We seemed to concur, agreeing to get together with one another throughout the summer in smaller pairings. In reality, we rarely did.

Seeing how we naturally dissipated exposed how we tried to set the stage for connectedness but most often failed to experience it. We appeared to be committed, yet we accepted taking extended summer breaks. Agreeing as a group to "take time-off" seemed innocent, but I could not deny it undermined any intent we otherwise had to forming strong relationships with one another. Finding myself without a church and small group, I clearly observed that all friendships ebb and flow, but the closest and most healthy do not adhere to a schedule and naturally gravitate towards togetherness.

I also noted that after leaving my last small group of two years, I did not readily carry those relationships with me. The experience revealed that, in at least some ways, I was committed to our meeting's day and time more than I was committed to the small group members. I had not realized it when I was a participant, but as a small group member, I was more faithful to honor our weekly gatherings than I was inclined to communicate with and intentionally care for the group members throughout the week apart from them.

I observed that I could attend a group long-term, extending well beyond the natural and fruitful duration of the relationships that had been conceived within it. This was proven when I stopped attending the group's weekly meetings and found that the relationships did not readily survive. The experience led me to question whether small groups consistently fostered life-giving relationships between individuals participating in them. If the fruit of the gatherings were organic, relationships from them would likely grow, regardless of the group itself.

I knew small groups could be beneficial, but finding myself without one, I discovered how much I expected them to be something more than a positive entity in my life. I inherently thought that the relationships within my small group would be marked by intimacy, friendship, consistency, and authenticity. As a result, I expected small group members to naturally experience magnetism. When we did not, I thought the small group was broken or unhealthy; meanwhile, I failed to consider that my expectations may be.

Beyond thinking that small groups naturally fostered intimacy, I also believed relational connectedness resulted from a substantial investment of time. Because of that belief, I continued to frequent small groups even when they felt forced or awkward. I thought that relationships within the group would eventually mature and grow more comfortable in time. While they did develop to a degree, in my experience they did not readily thrive. This explained how I could invest a long time with a group and never develop a prevailing friendship that I would take with me even if I left.

I began to reconsider my perceptions about Christian community, as several of my former church leaders had often stressed the importance of it in the life of every believer. I agreed with their notion, but upon finding myself without a church home, I discovered that *community* had assumed some static meaning in my mind—that it was marked by committed and calculated gatherings with consistent participants. As a result, I realized how much I believed small groups were God's primary means for fostering a sense of community in the life of every Christian. Thus, I had come to rely on church leaders to provide me with community rather than trusting God to form it in my life through his way and time.

As I learned to give greater credibility to my experiences in small groups, I stopped perceiving them as indispensable. Though small groups had always felt imperative to me, I was finally able to be honest with myself and acknowledge that I did not regularly find their fruit essential. Additionally, I embraced a broader definition of Christian community, recognizing it was attainable apart from regular participation in a small group. I acknowledged that "small groups" were man-made and constructed from a model. Though predominant among many congregations, the "one-size fits all" approach did not truly work, and I was not obligated to pretend that it did. Recognizing this even as I visited new church bodies, I no longer sought a small group but ceased looking for one. That decision helped end my learned belief that they were the source of community within the greater body of Christ. Fostering faith-based relationships became a greater priority to me while I placed less importance on their format and setting.

Finally, I saw greater significance in trusting God to grow relationships in my life, accepting the fact that local churches would always maintain limited ability to aid his hand. I embraced a certain reality I never wanted to acknowledge in the past. Scheduled meetings among Christians are easy to coordinate but interpersonal connections are not. Facing this truth freed me from lofty expectations I had placed on small groups, as if authentic encounters regularly sprouted from defined gatherings on particular days with predetermined people.

Today, I still value studying God's word collectively while having fellowship in my life, but I no longer fear my personal absence from a weekly event entitled "small group." I had thought that failing to attend weekly small group meetings would cause me to miss out on walking with Christ in the company of others. Now I recognize that longing for Christ-centered fellowship and fostering it is far more important than the specific form it assumes or label it carries. And I have developed greater confidence that God will sustain such relationships as long as he sees fit, even through the summer months and in the absence of sanction or title.

Chapter 12

RELATIONSHIPS

The most beautiful discovery true friends make is that they can grow separately without growing apart.

Elizabeth Foley

I know my neighbors.

As a Christian, I traversed years of adulthood expecting to meet my closest friends through whatever church I attended. After all, apart from a from a full-time job, my church life occupied the most consistent chunks of my time. However, particularly when I rounded the corner into my thirties, I felt a relational void in my life.

The most cherished friendships I had developed in my early twenties had been hijacked. My friends were experiencing new seasons of life and were overwhelmed by subsequent and mushrooming responsibilities. I felt friendships fade as my closest confidants became spread apart by miles and spread thin in their roles as wife and mother. As a twenty-something then thirty-something single person, facing distance in friendships due to newly forming family lives seemed normal, but my lingering loneliness did not.

Upon departing from Fairview Church, I assessed the totality of substantial friendships in my life. First, I observed that leaving a church home, even one I attended for 7 years, did not result in losing several significant relationships (because I didn't have but a few close friends during the tenure in which I was a member). In some ways, I grieved the absence of friends that I wished I had made at Fairview. In other ways, I felt sad knowing that my failure to form lasting friendships at the church was not due to a lack of trying.

Looking at the situation as objectively as I could, I faced the fact that I had exhausted a great deal of emotional energy believing significant friendships were a natural byproduct of a consistent church life. Meanwhile, I had done very little in attempting to foster relationships outside that arena. I discounted my ability to make friends through avenues other than the church, largely because I assumed the church was God's predominant path for developing friendships. As a result, I had failed to open my eyes to God's broader direction and activity in my life, other ways he may have satisfied my relational desires.

After leaving Fairview, I naturally found myself with more time and margin in my life, and I experienced a surprising openness to meet others, regardless of a given relationship's backdrop. I also discovered a new desire to invest effort and energy into people within my neighborhood. Seeking to engage neighbors was somewhat uncharted territory for me, and the thought was both exciting and terrifying.

Though difficult to admit, for several years and at many addresses I called home, I simply lived as if I was blind to the majority of my neighbors. I did not see apathy towards my neighbors as being Christian-like, but I was also not terribly convicted about it. In retrospect, I realize I had not considered investing a great deal of time getting to know my neighbors because I viewed my fellow church members as somehow being more divinely authored in my life than those in my subdivision.

I believed relationships birthed within the church were, shall I say, "utmost" providential. Befriending people within the church guaranteed some similarity–and to me, the most important kind. Meanwhile, I assumed friendships budding from church buildings were apt to be the closest and would happen with greatest ease, a perception that I held close in heart though it rarely transcended my reality. Still, if only in my imagination, relationships flowing from the church seemed to be most natural.

While I maintained some faith that I could grow to know my neighbors as friends, individuals at my church would always be *family* on account of our shared faith in Christ. I recognized that some neighbors could also be Christians, but I largely assumed they were not.

Because I assumed my neighbors adhered to a different religious view, electing not to engage them revealed how I valued the content of conversation and the personal satisfaction it provided me more than I appreciated the person with whom I traded the encounter. I prized common ground more than I prioritized the person in front of me. So even though I identified as a follower of Jesus, I did not relate to my neighbors as he would.

Getting to know neighbors felt risky in my mind because of the unknown. *What would we talk about?* I might wonder. I suspected conversations might hang in mid-air, so I judged or devalued interactions without ever entertaining them. I never considered that God's presence in the midst of two people could actually be just as valuable as conversation about him.

Before finding myself without a church home, I looked for friendships within my church so I could be assured that Jesus was a known factor, safe grounds for conversation and inherently preeminent. In some ways, this proved I cared more to share company with Christians and talk about God than represent him. Of course, I did not consider such a notion until I found myself outside of Fairview, along with a surprising interest to discover and know new people, particularly my neighbors.

As I stepped more deliberately into the streets around me, I clearly saw that during my years as a member of many local churches, I regularly discredited the depth of relationship I could share with people outside an explicitly Christian context. But in the absence of a church home, I noticed that I no longer reserved my relational attention to those within a congregation. Being more emotionally and mentally available, I found myself engaging and caring about others increasingly, especially those outside an ascribed church building.

In the end, several families on my street proved to be

incredibly warm, dynamic, and refreshing people, and I swiftly became a recipient of their kindnesses. I also became thankful for the change I saw in myself as I seized opportunities to know a handful of neighbors, a few lovely ladies I now consider friends.

I have non-Christian friends.

As a Christian, I have always known that I am supposed to love everyone and that I am supposed to be "in the world but not of it." But frankly, apart from going to work during my years in corporate America, I pretty much hid from "the world." I knew I wasn't supposed to live in a bubble, but I consistently cloistered myself with other Christians. While I was not justified, I maintained my reasons.

First, I separated myself from the masses because I have always been drawn to deep friendships. If I am in a situation where small talk is required, I will soon be searching for the door. In wanting to form meaningful relationships with other people, I had always maintained that shared-faith in Jesus Christ was the most essential element. In turn, if our Savior was not shared, then I felt conversation was left to what was superficial.

My second reason for relationally cloistering myself with other Christians was because I had a long-standing fear of liberals. While embarrassing to confess, I pretty much lumped all non-Christians into a relatively liberally labeled pool of people. Though I am not sure why I made such sweeping generalities, by doing so, I dodged potential relationships with people who professed different beliefs about God than I held to be true.

I behaved this way because I could not conceive that close friendships could exist where common belief in Jesus did not. I firmly believed the strongest bonds between individuals could only be formed through common ground, and for me the belief in Jesus Christ was largely the definition. Sharing faith in Jesus essentially became more significant than embodying the principles he taught. Jesus engaged the woman at the well; I think for a good part of my Christian life, I would have ignored her.

Beyond prioritizing what I deemed significant in conversation, I sought to cultivate friendships with Christians because I cowered at the idea of disagreeing with others. I assumed any lengthy conversations with non-Christians would eventually result in a focus on personal differences. Therefore, I envisioned dialogue being divisive before ever opening my mouth. Safer than risking uncomfortable conversations, I simply avoided the people I perceived likely to engage in them.

However, upon having no church home, my tune unexpectedly changed and so did my default approach to others. I became more intentional with those in my immediate surroundings and found myself open to new relationships no matter where they originated and regardless if those relationships were rooted in a shared faith. I shocked myself on account of the expansion that I experienced in the relational landscape of my life. Moreover, I was pleasantly surprised at small differences I saw in myself each day as I was more engaged with individuals at the grocery store and those who changed my oil.

As I interacted with others in any given scenario, I more naturally assumed an inherent human comradery concerning normal things of life. I expected to find more similarities with strangers than differences. I avoided less and said *hello* more. Meanwhile, issues of faith fell from the forefront of my mind. As never before, I first desired to know individuals than know what they believed.

I began to enjoy new people I met without pre-screening them to assess their beliefs about God. Meanwhile, I was more willing to "go the distance" with others in friendship, regardless of differences, particularly those of personal faith. I was pleasantly surprised to find that as long as two people had mutual interests and the relationship appeared to be reciprocal, friendships grew despite differences in religious beliefs or otherwise.

I learned along the way that I should not have been hesitant to embrace friendships with non-Christians because individuals determined to focus on divisive things are few. I also discovered it is possible to share many heartfelt experiences and grow close to others, even if the faith that frames those experiences runs on separate tracks. In a new way, I came to understand how common ground can serve as the glue between two people more than unique or opposing beliefs might threaten to repel them.

Not long after leaving my church home, I found out that Catherine, a long-term friend of mine, was in an abusive marriage. We were close confidants before she wed and had enjoyed participating in Christian gatherings and Bible studies together. I learned about the abuse after she had been married for more than ten years. When I found out, I had no frame of context for it and felt emotionally devastated. I was particularly overwhelmed by the newfound truth of Catherine's situation because I had wrongly believed she shared a loving, peaceful, and "Christian" marriage with her husband of many years.

About the time I discovered the news about Catherine, I was in the infant stages of getting to know a new friend. I had spent time with Beth only once before, but as we sat in oversized chairs at a local coffee shop, she listened with care as I poured out my feelings of despair concerning Catherine. My relationship with Beth was barely budding, and though she was not a Christian, she was the perfect person to sit across from me as I gushed from my grief-stricken heart.

After my verbal vomiting ceased, Beth opened up and immediately shared how she was subject to domestic abuse in her first marriage. I was encouraged as she spoke with wisdom from her own life and experiences as a victim. The tremendous and timely insight from my non-Christian friend felt like a gift from God; her words helped to ease my pain and equip me to be a better friend to Catherine.

Parting ways with Beth that day, I felt grateful and also humbled. I experienced a sense of relational significance and connection with her, something so sincere and unexpected. God comforted me through our visit, even though I was not completely sure whether Beth believed in God. She helped me tremendously as I grieved Catherine's abusive situation, but I about stopped in my tracks upon realizing I nearly never gave her the opportunity.

I first met Beth through a local event that had been established through Meetup.com. Upon sitting down at the first gathering, each woman offered her name and shared a brief description about herself. When it was her turn, Beth introduced herself and did not withhold the fact she was liberal, a word she chose to describe herself.

As soon as I heard her use the word *liberal*, I silently freaked out. In the first moments of my internal processing, I felt certain Beth and I had to be hugely different. Wondering if she could ever be a friend of any measure, I questioned how fitting such a friendship could be. Yet, in a few more minutes of her company, I was so struck by Beth's desire to love others, do good, and create relational bridges regardless of personal differences that I fell in love. I fell in love with a liberal. I didn't even know that was possible.

Though conflicting schedules and circumstances often caused our coffee dates to be sparse, my relationship with Beth naturally blossomed despite our differences. She made me laugh. She made me think about life. I learned from her. And as I continued to grieve Catherine's situation, Beth and I commiserated at times how domestic abuse had left an unwanted impression on our lives and hearts.

Meanwhile, a great irony transpired soon after meeting Beth, my loving, liberal, non-Christian friend. When I asked about her children, she shared with me that as a young adult, her step-son had become a conservative Christian. He went on to join a prominent megachurch in his city, a large metropolis within a neighboring state.

Beth explained how after he became a Christian, he retreated from his mom, dad, her, and his sister, his only sibling. Beth and her husband sought to maintain the relationship. For ten years, they continued to send gifts and cards to their son and his family in honor of birthdays and special occasions. Being met with silence in response, Beth said she and her husband eventually suspended their efforts.

I sat quietly and listened. Any interpersonal differences that arose as a result of her step-son's newfound faith had not been an obstacle for my friend and her husband. They simply loved their son and wanted to enjoy and embrace an ongoing relationship with him and his family. When I asked, Beth assured me that no grand altercation, stark debate, or argument had occurred, causing some overt conflict in their relationship. Instead, her step-son had just seemed to silently retreat from the rest of the family.

I don't know Beth's step-son, so I cannot speculate the reason that he withdrew from his family members following his decision to become a Christian. But when Beth shared her step-son's choice to embrace a conservative Christian faith and described how he then distanced himself from those with different beliefs, I had two distinct thoughts. *He is missing out—and that used to be me.*

Chapter 13

CHURCH ≠ GOD

Nor is He worshiped with men's hands, as though He needed anything, since He gives to all life, breath, and all things.

Acts 17:25 (NKJV)

I do not blame the church for my loneliness.

I did not realize the host of ways I relied on the churches I attended until I found myself without one. In many ways I looked to my church family to satisfy certain needs in my life rather than looking to God.

As a young single woman, I was excited at the prospect of getting married, and I held high expectations that I would meet my future husband within my local church. While I waited for my future mate, I desired to find a few fast friends, ones I also anticipated meeting in my congregation. In my thirties, as a still-single Christian, I wanted to feel well-connected to a few fellow parishioners despite their growing families and crowded schedules. However, several such longings went unsatisfied.

As a result, I viewed the relational landscape of my life as "broken." While I believed God maintained the right to reserve specific seasons of solitude for his children, I could not conceive that any church member should feel as if loneliness was familiar. My relational desires seemed good and legitimate, wants the Lord would satisfy. Moreover, the church appeared capable of aiding God's hand and often seemed to complement God's sovereignty, particularly by the programs it created. Church leaders established and maintained programs that fostered opportunity for church members to grow in relationship with one another, some I faithfully participated in. However, despite different platforms or ministry opportunities to meet others, I found fault with the groups when the ones suited for me didn't *work* for me.

Surrounded by other congregants every weekend, I believed I was "the exception" in experiencing feelings of isolation. I assumed everyone else was very well "plugged-in" and relationally satisfied, that most other congregants were actual friends and not just friendly in passing. I imagined the relationships others shared reflected true depth, where they naturally gravitated towards one another outside of church sanctioned events. In short, I believed others were reaping relational fruit from the church's programs while I only found myself wanting to.

Being a committed Christian and church goer yet longing for deeper and more consistent relationships left me feeling disillusioned. I believed certain wants or needs, like significant and sustainable friendships, were universal among people. I also assumed the local church, being a reflection of God himself, would be capable to meet the relational desires of his children, mine included.

In my mind, the church was best suited to anticipate such needs and both strategically and successfully satisfy them. If wants remained unmet, responsibility fell on those relegated to fix them: the church, its programs and their leaders. And I rarely, if ever, saw the expectations I placed on the church's people and programs as presumptuous. In fact, many structures and ministries of the local churches I attended were seemingly established for the purpose of satisfying the desires of its people.

Youth groups, singles groups, pre-marital weekend events, newly married groups and empty nester groups all catered to varying ages and stages of church members. By and large, each local church seemed to anticipate the unique needs of its people while making preemptive strides to satisfy them. And because I believed various church programs were intended for my benefit, I naturally felt justified in judging the kind of job they were doing.

Beyond believing the church would inevitably solve my feelings of loneliness, I felt it naturally maintained the responsibility of doing so. I continually anticipated that relationships would materialize through the church I attended and the ministries it maintained. I failed to see my expectations as errant, until I left.

After leaving, I released the church of its responsibility for relational fruit in my life before ultimately recognizing that I had placed blame where it did not belong. I was also able to see that in some ways, I viewed the local church as "God," or at the very least, the foremost way in which the real God worked.

Ironically, after leaving Fairview, I became more at peace with the relational landscape of my life. Though my relationships did not necessarily change, I discovered a greater satisfaction regarding their current state. Loneliness didn't dissipate; I just no longer held a congregation liable for it. Instead of blaming the church for my relational wants, I saw them as part of God's greater will.

In the months following my departure, I grew to understand that loneliness was not a fault of the church or a responsibility in which it was mandated to cure. Current relationships, whether I deemed them satisfying or not, were a reflection of God's best, not indicative of the church's right or wrongdoing. The relationships in my life were by the Lord's design for better or worse. Unsatisfied desires I had previously thought were the byproduct of a system gone bad, I grew to accept as part of God's plan which was good.

Rather than being someone's or something's fault, I began to understand and more greatly accept loneliness as a providential and purposeful orchestration of the Lord. While I maintained a desire for new and significant friendships, I learned the higher goal was to rely on God as I accepted the presence or absence of those relationships in my life.

I do not see the church as God's "Duct tape."

Throughout my years as a congregant, as far as I was concerned, the larger the local church, the more I expected needs inside and outside of it to be satisfied by the congregation and its programs. After all, larger churches had more people spanning greater demographics as well as more resources. Meanwhile, I gravitated towards more sizeable church bodies though not on account of this reason; the belief or attitude was simply a byproduct of continuing to attend them.

Upon leaving Fairview, I saw more clearly how often I looked to the megachurch to provide hope and healing for an array of people or scenarios, simply on account of its size. Expecting local churches like Fairview to meet the needs of people seemed logical, but placing such expectations on the local church largely led me to forget that God is bigger than His body. Because I believed that local churches were inherently responsible to help solve an array of personal and public issues, my view and understanding of the Lord grew to be quite limited.

A year and a half after Steve and I married, we fostered a teenager named Holly. Once after a half-day of school and with our permission, Holly went home with her friend, Natalie. We didn't know it at the time, but Holly's friend was essentially homeless. Estranged from her parents who lived in two different states, Natalie was living with another classmate's family. Following a half-day of school, the pair intended to have an afternoon of fun, but early in the afternoon, Holly unexpectedly called my husband in a frenzy.

Steve didn't know what was wrong, but Holly conveyed that he had to pick her up immediately. Steve had been working from home and promptly left for Natalie's house. Upon arriving, Natalie was having an altercation, arguing with the family she lived with. Observing the drama, Steve realized everyone needed to calm down, so he suggested the girls have a sleepover at our home for the night. Everyone agreed to his suggestion, and it was simple for Natalie to slip into the car because the family had already packed her suitcase.

Natalie stayed the night with us, and all was calm. Thinking everything would be better the next morning, Steve called the family to let them know that we would be bringing Natalie home. To our shock, the couple promptly and politely told him over the phone that she was not welcome back to their house. Overnight, we had somehow inherited a homeless teenager.

Not knowing what to do, I called our social worker through foster care. Upon answering, she wanted to help, but because Natalie had never been in the foster care program previously and because she was already eighteen, our social worker explained that the county was unable to assist her. As we hung up the phone, I went into a frenzy.

My husband and I were somewhat familiar with fostering, but we were ill-equipped to handle homelessness. Our daughter's friend attended school thirty-minutes away from our home and in the opposite direction of my full-time job which was located much closer to her school than Steve's office. I confess I was not thrilled at the idea of Natalie staying with us, but in my mind, the mere logistics of the situation deemed it an impossibility. Taking her to school every morning and driving to work would require nearly an hour and a half of time. Besides, I was not sure how Natalie would get home because classes dismissed sometime after 2:00 p.m. and I worked until 5:00 p.m.

I was wrought with despair, not knowing what to do. My sense of hope came when I recalled a certain church that I believed might be able to help. Having driven through the area a few times in the past, I remembered a sizeable church with a nice, newer building relatively close to Natalie's school. I found the name of the church and started placing frantic calls, hoping someone would answer or return my messages even though it was Saturday.

Hours later I received a call from a church official. I explained the situation and asked if he might know of a family that lived near Natalie's school, one that might be willing to host her, at least until graduation. At the time, it was the first week of March and graduation was only a handful of weeks away. I realized the request was quite out of the norm, but housing a homeless girl for a few weeks seemed like a Christian thing to do.

I had barely finished explaining the situation when, to my surprise, the man flatly replied, "We have no program for that, and besides, I would never feel comfortable asking one of our congregants to do that." With his response still hanging in the air, the conversation was over. Standing alone in the driveway, I was a bit dizzy and completely dumbfounded. I confess I was also irate.

Maybe some of my anger and frustration was justified, but the conversation with the man was one encounter of failed expectations that God would not waste. He used my disappointment and dejection to open my eyes, allowing me to see how I inherently placed reliance on the local church to remedy broken situations. I had not realized it, but I often equated the local church with God, thinking they were much the same.

Through the desperate experience with Natalie, God showed me how I ultimately looked to churches for answers, solutions he held in his hands. Expecting a church body to be Christ-like was understandable, but I was wrong to believe any church body would hold the same perfect power, love and means as Christ to satisfy a given need.

Witnessing a local church fail to respond to a real and urgent need or even attempt to was a circumstance God used to expose how I had long presumed upon him through his church. Recognizing my inherent dependence on God's local churches helped me to see that my perspectives needed to change. I had too easily forgotten that sometimes Christians prove unavailable or unwilling to help; other times, they may not be the people God would prefer to work through. In turn, I began to see God as God, recognizing that he is the Lord of local churches and at times chooses to meet the needs of hurting people without a congregation's involvement.

Expecting God's answers to be found solely within my church or the congregation closest to the current issue at hand was wrong thinking on my part. Through my disappointment, God revealed my misperceptions and how I believed that the church had failed me. The Lord used the opportunity to teach me that he remedies hardships his way, through whom he deems best. God began assuming a greater throne in my life, apart from his body. Moreover, he has taught me to rest, trusting that the person bringing the petition and any resulting answer, ultimately belong to him.

Chapter 14

GIVING

So let each one give as he purposes in his heart, not grudgingly or of necessity; for God loves a cheerful giver.

2 Corinthians 9:7 (NKJV)

I am conscious about my motivation for giving.

Through my years as a Christian, I was a slow and hesitant giver. For me, giving was largely a learned practice. I knew I was supposed to be a cheerful giver (2 Corinthians 9:7), but the joy of it did not come easily. Still, I grew to faithfully support the congregations I attended.

In the past when I left a church, I sometimes gave to that congregation until I found a new one. When I left Fairview, I elected not to because I was leaving for reasons specifically regarding fiscal decisions the church was making. Still, I cared about it and had given to Fairview regularly, over the course of several years.

After leaving the church, my inclination to give remained, but I was newly confronted with the motivation behind my desire. While I continued to visit churches in hopes of finding a new congregation, I usually elected not to put money in their offering plates. Simply speaking, I wasn't compelled to give to congregations I knew virtually nothing about. Though my decision not to give was arguably understandable, I experienced an increasing sense of guilt regarding it and found myself failing to comprehend why.

Observing my concerned conscience, I meditated on

my years of giving. In turn, I saw how my motivations had historically been unhealthy. Writing a check and having an offering plate in which to drop it felt like a necessary experience and responsibility as a Christian. This way of giving had become an inherent exercise, and not carrying it out felt as though I was leaving a fundamental practice of my faith outstanding. However, in not placing money into a passed plate, I did not feel as though I were being robbed of a privilege but negligent of a duty.

The guilt I felt over not contributing to an offering revealed that, even if I had put something in the plate, my motives were lacking. Seeking to get to the root of the matter, I was gentle with myself and let offering plates bypass me as I sorted out my motivations. My intent was not to cease being charitable, but to stop succumbing to guilt when I was not. In letting go of guilt, I could address my reasons for giving, what they had been and what they might grow to be.

With my conscience eased, I was better able to examine my habits. Historically, I waited to reach for my checkbook until the last possible minute, right before heading to services. And sometimes, I was prone to forget my check altogether. In the rare times I caught myself thinking about it a day or two before the service, I immediately told myself, *I'll write out a check later.* My mode of operation exposed that my giving was largely an afterthought. Frankly, I demonstrated less of a free will and more of a tight grip.

I gave regularly but made myself do it more than I found myself wanting to. I side-stepped the matter in large part when I decided to enroll in an auto-draft payment through the church's website. Electing to give electronically cured my conscience because it was a more foolproof way of attaining consistency. That decision remedied my unfaithfulness, but it never addressed my motivation. I only began to examine my heart when my auto-draft ceased, particularly upon my termination and exit from Fairview.

Giving substantial amounts of money to the church was not easy, but previously, the issue of greatest importance was that I proved faithful in doing it. Consistency in the exercise warded off guilt more than it was fueled by delight. Experiencing true joy through giving felt like a spiritual gift imparted to some Christians while remaining more absent in others. Simply speaking, I believed I fell into the latter category and did not anticipate that changing. So, I sought to give faithfully which I believed was pleasing to God, but I accepted or dismissed the heart in which I did it.

In time, I became sensitive to my reasons for giving. Before, I sometimes chose to be charitable even when my heart was not inclined. Now, I sometimes elect not to share financial resources simply because I do not affirm the attitude in which I would be doing so. Regardless if I give or not, I have desired to become more in tune with my heart's posture in a given transaction. Additionally, I have become conscious of potential sin on the opposite side of any chance to be charitable. If I elect not to give when an opportunity arises, I may fail to meet a certain brother's need. But if I do give, I may harbor a rotten attitude in the process.

Knowing the motivation behind my giving has become more important to me than when certain allotted funds were on auto-draft. While I did not become a person who gives or doesn't based solely on feelings, I did become one who, at times, yields to the inclination of my heart over honoring the act itself. More than anything, I became cognizant of not wanting to contribute money out of a sense of duty because for me, giving had become requisite to my faith rather than a practice of privilege. I just hadn't recognized the difference nor given weight to its importance.

I am mindful about the end result of my giving.

Throughout my years as a Christian, giving away finances rarely felt like a moving or personal experience. Over the years, I did not meditate on the money I gave to congregations nor readily considered its fruit. In donating to a church, I gave somewhat with blind eyes and a heart of trust. I naturally felt confident that the gifts in the offering plate were gathered for a congregant to count, then dispersed wisely by the church's leaders.

I felt satisfied trusting the stewardship of others, knowing that what I gave partially supported the church's operation. Knowing that a portion of my financial gifts sustained the church building and another part helped pay each pastor was reasonable in my mind. Anything or anyone else my giving supported was largely at the leaders' discretion, and this arrangement was acceptable to me and comfortable to my Christian conscience.

The good from my giving may have extended well beyond each church I attended, but I did not know how the lives of others were being enriched through my benevolence. I was not acquainted with the missionaries I was aiding or the projects I might be supporting. I gave with full confidence in the stewardship of others and only periodically looked at pie charts representing budgets. I maintained a sense of contentment in my giving and its ultimate uses, trusting my investment and its distribution even if I could not discern the fruits of it with my own eyes.

Only when I worked as a church employee did I readily consider that churches—those I had attended and the one where I worked—likely spent money in ways I deemed inappropriate. I hadn't entertained this notion until I experienced it as a reality, for instance, when I learned that Fairview had hired a third-party to manage the church's financial campaigns. The experience showed me that, as a congregant, I never contemplated how my current giving could also be supporting a church's unwise, but previously executed, financial decision. After Fairview's vote, I elected to leave, choosing not to morally or monetarily support its direction. However, when I joined Fairview, I never inquired about the church's historical choices and correlating debts. In failing to ask, I demonstrated a lack of wisdom about my money's ultimate use. I felt responsible to give but demonstrated little care in how it was spent.

Gaining broader perspectives as a church employee, I increasingly considered the end result of my giving, and my duty to know about it. Realizing that I had never been mindful about the fruits of my giving as a congregant, I resolved that when I gave money in the future, I would aim to better comprehend its use. Learning more details about how my gifts were spent became a newfound desire and a newly felt responsibility.

Meanwhile, in the absence of a new church home, I grew motivated to consider other contexts in which I could be charitable. Previously, nearly all the money I donated each year went to my local congregation. Church leaders then assumed responsibility for spending it to satisfy specific needs *they* deemed most appropriate. Not having a church, I felt empowered to discover that I maintained the same potential to alleviate needs, despite being the lone individual to identify, define or substantiate them.

During this time, I took a trip to see my parents. Upon landing at the airport, I climbed into an Uber to travel the remaining eighty miles. As the driver eased onto the expressway, I felt a bit anxious because the car's transmission felt funny, seemingly sick. Apparently oblivious, my driver concentrated on the road ahead, sharing in great detail about the love he had for his wife. The two were first generation immigrants, trying to make a living in the United States which he indicated was nearly impossible in their homeland.

My driver explained he was the sole person in his family working because his wife was caring for their newborn in addition to her disabled brother, a young man visiting them for the summer. He shared honestly, even confessing insecurities about his limited ability to interact and care for his crippled brother-in-law because of his extensive impairments. The driver safely delivered me to my parents' home, meanwhile moving my heart. In my estimation, I saw my car ride as an opportunity to extend a helping hand to a fellow human being. Upon arriving, I left him a tip almost as much as the fare.

Being overly generous with the Uber driver left me feeling as though my giving had been especially personal, something I had rarely experienced before. In the years I had given primarily to a congregation, I hardly ever looked into the eyes of individuals impacted by the financial resources I had given. Though giving to former church bodies was not inconsequential, the act rarely felt meaningful because I did it sitting in a pew.

Recognizing opportunities to give and be a blessing to others became an increasing desire, regardless of my financial gifts to a local church. I found myself wanting to be poised to give, should a fitting opportunity arise. I am not sure if my increased desire to give resulted in a greater love of people or the other way around, but regardless, both grew considerably.

The pleasure I experienced in giving became more normative. However, I also felt sad knowing I had missed some measure of joy in my Christian walk previously, particularly in not resolving to see the good from my giving more often. Though I never set out to give in ways that were largely outside the context of a congregation, the experience was a byproduct of finding myself without a church home. While unintentional, the experience inevitably bore fruit in my life. I helped different people than I otherwise would have, aided others more directly, and experienced a new joy in the process. Finally, I learned to consider who or what my giving was impacting, something I had rarely asked myself in all my years as a Christian.

◆◆◆

I see a greater relationship between giving and evangelism.

If someone had asked me a short time ago if giving and evangelism were connected, I would have answered, "Loosely." I would have said that congregations' financial gifts helped sustain church buildings where non-Christians could visit worship services and hear the gospel of Jesus Christ. Or I might have said that churches' financial benevolence provided aid to hurting people, locally and internationally. Those recipients may come to know Christ as the gospel is shared with them in conjunction with receiving help to meet their physical needs.

Without having a church home, giving to others in more personal and direct ways eventually led to a shift in my view of evangelism. Previously, I had always felt that evangelism was best done by professionals (i.e. the Pastor). I regret, therefore, treating evangelism foremost as an exercise where I tried to bring non-Christians to a weekend church service.

I felt that, especially while I attended Fairview Church, we had one of the best teaching pastors in the country. If anyone was going to understand their need for Jesus and the miraculous love he offered, hearing a sermon as part of our pastor's captive audience would bring the highest odds. His message was bound to be compelling to the intellect and provoking to the heart, and every visitor would hear their need for salvation through Jesus Christ within one of Fairview's 75-minute services. Meanwhile, I saw my primary role in the evangelistic process as inviting non-Christians to come.

However, as the landscape of my giving changed, so did my attitude towards evangelism. I began to see myself as being more intricately inserted into the lives of others than I had before, specifically as a conduit to Christ. Instead of feeling compelled to introduce others to my Savior overtly through a sermon, I felt a greater inclination to show Jesus to others, if even covertly, by having a more charitable heart.

Prior to assuming greater responsibility in evangelism, I saw little relationship between spending money and sharing the gospel. As far as financial giving, I felt my fiduciary responsibility as a Christian was largely satisfied upon giving to the church in which I was a member. But I found Christ's call to help others as unto Him (Matthew 25:35-40) to be newly significant and personal when I found myself without a church to call home. I saw giving as a much wider opportunity to invest in God's kingdom, and I grew to respect that my generosity had a much broader relationship to evangelism than I had previously acknowledged.

I became convicted that I had more strongly believed others would discover Jesus by hearing my pastor preach than I expected they might encounter Jesus in me, at least in part, by adopting greater generosity as a way of life. I began to understand that by helping to meet the needs of others or simply giving more freely, I could better represent the love of Jesus tangibly to others which might also result in them asking about my motivation.

    When I give to others now, I aim to do so without expectation. However, I believe I am sharing the love of Christ while potentially cultivating curiosity in others about him. Regardless if any person sees Christ behind my giving, I rest knowing that God sees my gift and that he remains the final recipient, as my giving is ultimately unto him.

Chapter 15

CHURCH

> *One hundred religious persons knit into a unit by careful organization do not constitute a church any more than eleven dead men make a football team. The first requisite is life, always.*
>
> AW Tozer

My view of *church* has changed, and so has my vocabulary surrounding it.

When I left my church and job, I felt like a displaced Christian. While it would have been nice to land immediately in a new local body of believers, no insta-church-family was waiting to receive me. Instead, I felt nomadic. Finding myself in a wandering way, I became ever mindful of the word *church* as I considered my relationship to it and my status as part of it. In turn, I began to consider the kinds of conversations I regularly had with others about church. I often shared dialogue about church life and posed questions like, "What church do you attend? Where is your church? We are new to the area. Do you like your church?"

In meditating on the word, I realized that the question: *Where is your church?* is flawed by definition because buildings exist at crossroads, but churches do not. Yet for decades, I had conversations like these regularly and thought nothing of them. I also never readily considered God's description of his church (e.g. Ephesians 2:19-22) in comparison to how I was using the word. I realized my relationship to the church was inherently broken because I was living out of a flawed understanding of its meaning.

Moreover, I failed to see that how I used the word *church* directly (yet subconsciously) impacted how I related to it. In the subconscious part of my mind and in the predominance of my vocabulary, church was not foremost defined as members of a family but as a weekend service or program. In my heart, I believed God's church was alive, but my speech surrounding it only framed that which was inanimate. I knew in one sense that the church was God's people, but I did not most commonly relate to or speak about it in that way.

In conversation with others, I most often used the word *church* to mean *weekend services*. Week after week, I made reference to worship programs and specifically my or my friends' participation in them. Based on my words, church was comprised of many things, including music, Sunday School and sermons. Though I spoke as if it had many components, I hardly ever spoke as if it was a family, in which I was a part.

"How was church last weekend?" I often asked my friends. In turn, I listened as they told me the highlights concerning the hour or two that they occupied their respective church buildings. The question, a common one among me and other Christians, invited feedback about a sermon, their children's activities, or worship songs that were sung. The subject of the inquiry was an event, not a people; in other words, my question was not concerning the state of those within the church building and the health of their familial relationship but an assessment of the time they spent observing certain activities together.

While not as common, I did occasionally see *church* as a body or group of people. I was most cognizant of relating to the church as a group of God's children whenever I sought to become a member of a local congregation. During any period of time when I found myself without a church home, I felt compelled to find a new one; I wanted a new body, or family, in which to belong. However, seeing a new church as "the body" was short lived, as I usually chose my future body based on its teaching (biblically sound or not) and music (pleasing to me or not). In short, I desired to be in a family of faith, but oddly, I did not take ample time getting to know its people before choosing to settle into a church.

After leaving Fairview, I felt removed in heart and less than eager to engage in a search for a new congregation. Instead, I reflected on the components I had always used to assess churches during the different times I aspired to join a new one. I also reevaluated the factors I employed to gauge whether a church was favorable or not, or even legitimate.

Throughout my years as a Christian, I had largely believed a local church was only "real" if it had a unique and specific name, was registered as a 501(c)(3), and had a designated pastor. My perspectives changed when I realized that I was judging something that was not mine with a definition that was not God's. Previously, I had determined whether a church was credible or not based on my own biases–none of which was outlined in God's word. While my unit of measure was inaccurate, so was the subject I set out to assess. I focused on analyzing the validity of an entity, all the while overlooking the health or vibrancy of God's people within it, his actual church.

After discarding my wrong concepts of church, I weighed the sense of identity that I had always felt as a part of one. I realized that during my latter years at Fairview, I did not delight in my identity as a Christian as much as being one simultaneously attached to a very specific local church—particularly, a prestigious one. Only after leaving Fairview did I realize how much of my Christian identity was wrapped up in the particular church I attended. A few fellow church members had become friends, but I had more closely associated with *Fairview* on the church door than I did with any one person inside. My commitment to the church was deep and genuine, but I eventually acknowledged my commitment was foremost to an enterprise rather than a people or family. I felt my love and devotion to the church was genuine, but after leaving Fairview I saw how my commitment to its activities trumped my faithfulness to its people. My sense of allegiance was foremost tied to particular days and times, a commitment to church services and small groups, more than the people with whom I sat elbow-to-elbow.

As I began to see God's church more accurately and better understood my relationship to it, I sought repairs in how I related to it. I became more sensitive when speaking about a church body, particularly in making reference to whose it was. Before, I would regularly and casually use phrases like "my church" or "your church." Because the word *church* came to encompass a new meaning in my heart, I became more conscientious about God's lordship over his body, avoiding such phrases altogether. I also stopped saying that "I went to church" over a given weekend. Instead, I would speak in terms of participating in a service, fellowship or gathering.

Beyond speaking about God's church and relating to it differently, I grew to increasingly embrace its various forms. Holding a more biblically based concept of *church*, I understood that Christians assembling together for weekend services was not the only manifestation of God's body; rather, God's church was represented wherever His people gathered. I also assessed my attitude concerning the different forms the body of Christ might assume. Instead of deeming participation in a church service as inherently holy, I came to believe that Christians gathering outside of church buildings could be exhibiting God's body of believers in a manner just as sacred.

Church shifted in my mind from an organization and its ongoing activities to a people. I also came to believe that the vibrancy of a congregation was not tied foremost to the commitment of its members to attend services week over week. Instead, I saw the health of a church as being rooted in relationships. More specifically, I believed the frequency of interpersonal engagement was indicative of a church's health, particularly how often the interactions transpired apart from formally sanctioned gatherings.

◆◆◆

I do not love the local church more than God's greater Church.

If someone had asked me in college, after college, or when I attended Fairview Church, I would have told them in all of those places and at all of those times, "I love my church." Throughout each season of life, I attended a church that seemed most beneficial to me, for particular reasons in each respective time and city. And at each of those congregations, I would have said that I wished that the church I attended would grow.

I wanted non-Christians to become Christians, adding to the number of God's greater Church, but I also became excited at the prospect of new and old converts coming to the local church that I attended. Each church that I chose to call home had unique elements that I enjoyed, and I naturally wanted to share those things with others.

Esteeming my church body and maintaining a desire for others to enjoy it seemed normal to me. However, as I unexpectedly faced a season without an attachment to any particular church, my perspectives largely changed. Instead of seeing adoration for a local congregation as commonplace and benign, I began to see how love for a local church body could actually be an underlying sign of sickness.

Having left Fairview Church, I continued to visit a host of other local church bodies for many months. After attending one congregation somewhat regularly, I signed up for its yearly women's retreat. As I met and spoke with a few ladies from the church, each one offered rave reviews about the special annual event. Being an introvert, I was anxious as a newbie but hopeful about going, so I filled out the form and submitted my check. Several weeks later, the retreat weekend arrived, and I cautiously climbed into a car with a few women whom I had never met. As I buckled in and we backed out of my driveway, I peered out the window and wondered how we might encounter God during a weekend at an oversized beach house together.

I was still settling into my seat when the driver cordially asked, "How long have you been a member of the church?" I explained I was just a visitor at the church and did not currently belong to a particular congregation. I went on to share that Steve and I were most frequently visiting the church hosting the retreat and one other local congregation. In response, she exclaimed, "Oh great! We are going to have to show you how we are better than they are!"

I was shocked silent and immediately thought, *"Why better?"* I felt put-off by her church pride and instinctively wanted to get out of the car. Though I never wished to be a touchy person, I debated dialing an Uber even as we made our way down the expressway. Aborting the trip seemed preferable over staying with a woman holding a newly formed agenda–to get me to love her church and prefer it over another.

While I am sure she meant well, I strangely felt prey to her perspective. I had elected to go on the ladies' retreat because I wanted to grow closer to Christ and have a chance to know fellow Christians. As a visitor with no church to call home, the weekend at the beach was about God and a sense of eternal sisterhood, not about camaraderie concerning a particular congregation.

I felt offended about the exchange for much longer than I care to admit. I wrestled even longer with trying to understand why I could not seem to let it go. But in time, the truth of the situation struck me. *I was that woman.* I was the prideful pot calling the kettle black. In my Christian adulthood, I had assumed that exuberance for a local church body was normal and inherently acceptable among Christians. Apparently, I had forgotten the valuable observations I had taken from childhood; maintaining love for a specific local church could be harmful, and such affection could unearth a heart of competition within God's greater body.

The encounter was a tremendous lesson for me because it caused me to reevaluate my sense of personal loyalty and love for a local church body and how such devotion could directly or indirectly impact others, even negatively. For the first time, I contemplated how the love and pride I had held for my previous churches may have been observable and offensive to those around me. I also became aware of ways that my attitude, spoken or not, was less than loving towards fellow Christ-followers because I was often less interested in learning how they were communing with God and more interested in knowing the name of the church in which they engaged him.

The interaction on the way to the ladies' retreat helped me

see my own heart and attitudes more clearly. My former "church pride" fell into focus for what it was–sin. Having been offended on the way to the Christian retreat, I was ultimately able to discover a specific and personal trespass while realizing I was not isolated in being prone to commit it. I was among other Jesus-followers who did not love their local church as Christ did, but regarded them to some degree as *better*.

As a church nomad, I more clearly saw impure affections I had held towards previous church bodies I attended, adoration that was tainted by a root of arrogance. I also recognized how my attitude was not unique and being blind to its negative effects was easy. As a result, I became at least a little leery of Christians who oozed love for their local church bodies. My honesty may appear cynical to those who adore their church because they may see their affection as pure and good, but so had I.

Though I had long done the same, when someone else plugged their church to me at a time when I had no church to call my own, I no longer saw such advertising as innocuous. Instead, I pondered afresh that Jesus did not sell a congregation, belong to one local church, or favor a particular body of Christians. He simply sought to engage, love and serve others while teaching those around him to do the same.

In recent days, I am no longer preoccupied with learning which local body a Christian friend or stranger associates; moreover, I do not judge their decision based on what I believe is best. Instead, I am more interested in knowing they are experiencing God authentically.

Chapter 16

SCOPE

Christian brotherhood is not an ideal which we must realize; it is rather a reality created by God in Christ in which we may participate.

Dietrich Bonhoeffer

I dream of a cooperative Church.

One byproduct of being part of a megachurch was that I felt empowered. If one local church did a backpack drive to help meet the needs of one local school, Fairview Church's backpack drive could satisfy six. But after leaving Fairview, when I lost attachment to any particular church body, I began to get excited about something greater than the scope of a single supersized church.

I no longer saw any one congregation as being better or more influential than another. Instead, I began to wonder how great an impact would be felt in the community if local congregations labored together more cooperatively. I found myself wanting to see churches working and praying together, something I rarely daydreamed about previously. Though the idea was not altogether unique, such a reality seemed quite rare.

A few months after leaving Fairview, I became acquainted with a pastor of another local church. Not long after we met, he and I discussed our desire to see churches working together more deliberately. He explained how just the year before, his three-person church staff pounded the pavement prior to the National Day of Prayer. His team went to every church within a five-mile radius and personally invited their respective staff members to pray together on the forthcoming day earmarked for intercession (since we live in the Bible Belt, they had knocked on a lot of doors). The pastor said that on the National Day of Prayer, outside those from his staff, one church worker came to the prayer meeting he had orchestrated.

As the pastor shared, I was bewildered by his account and the lack of congregational comradery he had witnessed. So a few months later, as the National Day of Prayer approached again, I attempted something similar. I reached out to a handful of pastors, leaders, and church staff that I had met personally, if only once. Together, they represented about a half-dozen local church bodies.

I asked each of them just a few questions, "Do you know if any local church leaders are gathering together in prayer on the National Day of Prayer? If you do, may I join you? And if you don't know of any, would you and your staff like to work together to establish one?" Of the handful of church leaders and staff that I emailed my questions, none knew of an existing prayer meeting among local church leaders. And of those I invited to orchestrate one, a single church administrator and pastor came.

The scenario demonstrated an apparent lack of interest among church leaders to pray with one another, an observation that left me disappointed. The situation caused me to reflect on previous experiences with corporate prayer. I considered my long history as a member of a few local congregations as well as my handful of months without one. During my time as part of various church bodies, I noted that prayer was primarily a private act in my Christian life. Regardless of my faithfulness to pray personally, I rarely gathered with the church body to pray in unison for our congregation and surrounding community.

Moreover, I realized the desire to pray corporately was largely absent in my own heart because the lack of intercession throughout my years as a church member obviously had not bothered me. Because I was faithful to meet with other believers every week for church services, I did not give much thought to the context in which we gathered. Any absence of petitioning our Lord together, asking him to purify us and work through us, had largely failed to faze me.

However, upon leaving Fairview and ceasing church service attendance for a time, I found it interesting that I missed sermons a little and singing some more, but what I really craved was to find some Christian comrades and pray together. My desire for joint intercession did not result in prayer meetings in my living room, but I did find myself praying more often, if even alone. I also found a bit of solace through the use of *Voxer*, a certain app on my phone; I used it to pray more consistently with friends that also engaged its "walkie talkie" function. Moreover, I experienced greater pleasure in prayer than I had before. Praying with others more naturally and joyfully, I wondered what might happen if my new reality were not such a sparse one among Christians at large.

After leaving Fairview and noticing the sparseness of corporate prayer among God's people, I also observed how infrequently churches invested time together in other Christ-centered ways. I had not considered it before, but in all my years at various church bodies, I could not recall a single event or ministry where the church that I attended chose to combine its efforts with those of another congregation.

As a church member, interceding or working arm-in-arm with another congregation had never really crossed my mind. But in finding myself without a church home, I felt compelled that local churches should gravitate towards one another in love and in working together for the common good of the community. With a growing passion for partnership rolling through my veins, cooperative efforts and attitudes suddenly appeared absent from most local church bodies. While I had never paid attention to it previously, the seeming disunity bothered me.

I stopped and considered why churches were not aspiring to pray and work together intentionally and why I had never seen local church bodies as siloed before. At the very least, I acknowledged that I had been part of the problem. As a Christian who adored my respective church, I had never readily desired to labor with members of any church outside my own. Instead of seeing other congregations as part of God's greater body, as my brothers and sisters in Christ, I saw them as *different*. And the differences distracted me from our unity in Christ because I foremost saw them as contrary, not complimentary.

As a congregant of a local church body and as a Christian for decades, I had always observed a host of church buildings that lined the streets where I lived. The mass number of buildings did not move me as it ought, considering God's numerous followers gathering inside them. Rather, their differences perpetually jumped to the front of my mind. *Different* names. *Different* denominations. *Different* service times. *Different* races. *Different* demographics. *Different* kinds of buildings. *Different* pastoral styles. *Different* music. *Different* atmospheres. *Different* customs in services. Focusing instinctively on their dissimilarities led me to view God's local church bodies primarily as separate entities, not integral counterparts that comprised a whole.

However, succumbing to a season without a church home, I started to see the same stretch of churches around me with new eyes. I became amazed at how vast God's greater Church truly was as I considered how many local church bodies were within New Haven. I also became humbled upon conceiving the incredible potential at God's disposal. My new perspective led me to repeatedly contemplate, *What if…?* And the questions that arose in my mind naturally stirred my soul. *What if each congregation focused more outwardly and sought to work cooperatively and intentionally with other congregations? What might God accomplish through them? What if God's sons and daughters sought to love God's Church over any smaller portion of it? What impact would that have on a watching city? What if local church bodies served one another, sacrificed for one another, and joined forces with one another?*

If one local Christian body had Meals on Wheels, one had Divorce Care and another had Celebrate Recovery, what might happen if each church began actively sharing about their ministries, leveraging them together for the greater good of the community? What would it look like if each member of God's greater Church deliberately sought new friendships across local congregations, ones with established ministries that were consequential to the community, apart from their own? At the very least, laboring together across church bodies might draw a host of Christians into doors of churches they may not otherwise frequent.

Joining forces and reaching across congregations and denominations would foster a more united front among Christians in New Haven. The differences among congregations—their various sizes, racial and socioeconomic demographics, traditional or contemporary biases, music and instrumental preferences, and rote or freeform approaches— would be placed aside for the determined purpose of serving and loving others—together. The outward cohesion would impact onlookers positively for God as they witnessed churches' cooperative efforts. Apart from the impression left upon witnesses, the hearts of those working together would likely be moved. God's children might taste the fruit of increased unity, having gathered and learned from one another as members of a greater collective and cooperative family.

Chapter 17

PASTORS

I do not consecrate myself to be a missionary or preacher. I consecrate myself to God to do his will where I am, be it in school, office, or kitchen, or wherever he may, in his wisdom, send me.

Watchman Nee

My notion of *pastor* has changed.

Upon resigning from my job and leaving my church, I visited a handful of congregations over the course of several months. The extended span of time provided substantial opportunity for reflection about my walk with God. Finding myself in a season without a church home, I asked myself the question, *Who is my pastor?* which led me to then ask, *What is a pastor?*

In all of my years as a member of local churches, I believed that pastors possessed certain characteristics. One general belief I maintained was that the most credible pastors held a seminary degree from a biblical college. As I reflected on my concept of a pastor, I realized that my belief was skewed because God's designation of pastors preceded the construction of seminaries. As a result, I started to give more time to exploring my concept of pastors as well as my relationships with those who assumed the role.

If someone had asked me a few years ago to name all the pastors in my life, I would have listed the name of each person who maintained the title throughout the various congregations I attended. Each one was paid by the church and had a designated office with a name plate outside the door. My list would have included Christian "professionals," individuals who worked for God in a formal capacity and received financial compensation for doing so.

When I found myself without a church home for a longer stretch of time than I might have anticipated, I started to develop a slight insecurity about not having a pastor. I felt as though something was potentially amiss in my Christian walk, because I could not point to a particular person as "my" pastor. The sense of uneasiness I experienced over not having a minister in my life did not reveal that my heart was longing for a mentor that had gone missing—most of my pastors were not well acquainted with me and the details of my life. But the subtle angst did cause me to do some internal digging in order to find its cause.

First, I discovered how I perceived the position of pastor as superior to other jobs or functions within God's family. The Lord created his body with assorted members or distinguished parts. Though God differentiated them or their roles to some degree, he did not assign them varying worth. Still, I inherently viewed the position of pastor as especially noble or honorable. God did not establish echelons in his church family, but I had. The absence of a certain *role* in my life—not the absence of *relationship* with a person in such a role—led me to discover that I saw "stations" within God's body, and some of them as more worthy than others.

Beyond perceiving the role of *pastor* as some high office, I saw it as set apart for special individuals. The uncommon and curious nature of the job—that it required credentials few individuals ever satisfied by western Christianity's standards, and those who did received a paycheck to work for God "full-time" —only perpetuated my false notion that the function was an "elite" one. Moreover, my reverence for the role then led me to elevate the individuals operating in it.

Every other role in the church, I saw as imparted by God—a gift. But I believed the pastoral role was ascertained through man's efforts and accomplishments. Believing the role was achieved by man more than given by God, I inherently esteemed men who had "obtained" it. Because the American pastorate is largely satisfied by people holding specific collegiate credentials, I respected those who achieved the title, humbly aware of the sweat, blood and tears required to achieve it.

Additionally, thinking pastors were only found on stages or in sanctuaries revealed what a narrow view I had about them. I believed that formal education or a church's designated process of ordination were solid means for labeling someone as a pastor. During my years as a Christian, I would have said that "schooling" would have been the primary way to identify or substantiate someone as a pastor. However, I was rarely familiar with my pastors' education, when and where they completed a biblical education. I never inquired about it, because I knew they had to have been "ordained" or "installed" at some point, which was satisfaction enough for me that they were suitable for the job.

Thus, I assumed each pastor had authenticity and character that affirmed their function. As far as readiness for the role, because someone else had examined them in such a vein—seminary officials or elders and deacons—I maintained no sense of need or responsibility to do the same. I propagated a sense of blind trust through my acceptance of our relationship, even though its setting was primarily, if not exclusively, corporate in nature. I did not learn from them personally, through life—but publicly, from a pulpit. I thought nothing of this arrangement, and intently listened to their spoken lessons, meanwhile being unfamiliar with their lifestyle. The type of relationship I maintained with most of them was marked by formality, not familiarity.

Apart from being familiar with their cadence and the words my pastors taught, I had not been deeply acquainted with most of my pastors. They may have spoken eloquently about love, humility, and servitude, but in regards to most of them, I did not generally have opportunities to see such characteristics played out in their lives. Having a measure of relational distance between me and someone I considered to be my pastor was normal. Establishing a personal relationship with him—one real enough to witness his humanity—seemed both unrealistic and taboo.

The relatively distant and impersonal relationship I had with the majority of my pastors was not unique. Because each one ministered to a host of congregants, only a fraction of parishioners might know a given pastor intimately. Still, I inherently esteemed them as "special" individuals among the congregation. I held subconscious admiration for them because of their title, not some close-knit relationship we shared.

In most of the churches I had joined through the years, I did not expect to know the pastor intimately, given the size of even modest congregations. I saw a pastor's role as teaching in addition to caring for congregants in more personal ways. Though my interactions with pastors did not often extend beyond Sunday morning services, I imagined their personal influence would eventually touch my life in a more consistent and intimate way, maybe if I faced a season of hardship. However, when I encountered difficult times, I did not find myself dialing them at home or the church's office. Had I tried, they may have known my name, but nearly all of them would not have known particulars about my life or the street where I lived.

Not having a church in which I was intimately affiliated, I spent time thinking about qualities that were requisite and fitting for someone I considered to be a pastor. As I reflected, a pastor grew to mean something different than an official person "over" a congregation in which I was a part. The defining characteristics became less about the attainment of an ordination certificate, a title, or paid position. Instead, I found myself asking, *Who is pastoral is my life?* Oddly, my answer raised the bar in regards to who was qualified while instantaneously increasing the number of people it described.

Realizing I had known other men to live, act and love me pastorally without ever holding the title led me to believe many more are gifted by God in pastoring than are ordained by congregations. Several men may hold jobs as pastors and some may have been placed there by God, but I have come to think the Lord has many other members assuming the role despite never being given the title. After all, men who are functioning pastorally are inherently more concerned about the people they are caring for than what position they are fulfilling. In turn, I suspect several members of Christ's body are given by God to be pastors than are likely to identify as one.

Before finding myself without a church to call home, I had considered the pastors in my life to be trusted servants, but for the most part, I gave them my trust because of their title and what I thought to be true of them. Bearing witness to their integrity and authenticity did not feel necessary because I did not hold that my pastor had to "prove" himself to me in a particular way. In large part, I believed he already had, through his ordination and rapport with elders and deacons (ironically, individuals with whom I was often not familiar). Viewing my impersonal relationship with all of them as normative, I gave pastors my confidence without ever requiring them to earn it, an unparalleled gift considering most other relationships in my life.

Previously, I esteemed pastors more highly than other members of Christ's body. I now view God's people and their roles within his church without partiality. Instead, I understand that each member of the Lord's body is equally integral. Seeing God's members and their various forms with greater importance, I discovered that God's assignment for each church member is less significant than their commitment to work heartily in it for the welfare of the whole.

In seeking to love God well and live faithfully for him, I no longer ask, "Who is my pastor?" Instead, I aim to recognize the men who demonstrate pastoral care in my life. For me, the latter has become more important. Otherwise, I can maintain membership in a local congregation with a designated pastor to call my own, but his presence in my life may be somewhat inconsequential if I have no relationship with him.

———◆◆◆———

My Bible does not compete with pastors.

I have often thought that captivating and relevant teaching from a pulpit was difficult to find. Though I am not proud to admit it, I have attended a few churches largely because of their pastors, because they had a knack for consistently delivering engaging sermons. Without a doubt, Fairview Church was one. I enjoyed our pastor's teaching a great deal, often watching his sermons on-line in addition to those I observed during weekend services. I sometimes questioned what would happen if our lead pastor were struck by illness or tragedy, no longer able to assume a position behind the pulpit. His teaching ability was a significant reason I chose to attend the church, a fact that was confirmed each time I considered the hypothetical scenario.

Upon leaving Fairview, I realized how much I had injected a host of other people into my relationship with God. While I did commune with God directly through the Bible and prayer, I also regularly reached for devotional books by my favorite authors and watched portions of on-line sermons by my favorite pastors. At the time, I saw them as mere resources and tools, and I would have told anyone who questioned me concerning them that they were peripheral in my Christian life.

However, God showed me how central to my Christianity I had allowed them to become. The frequency in which I reached for "supplemental tools" was a strong indication of my reliance on them. On average, I read about ten Christian books annually. Meanwhile, nearly every day of the week, I listened to 15-30 minutes of an on-line sermon, most often by a pastor whose teaching I loved or ones that came recommended to me. And on the days when I considered myself most fortunate, the 15 or 30-minute measure of time would extend to 45-minutes or more.

Watching sermons was not altogether bad for my faith journey. However, the time I invested in them was much greater than the Christ-like fruit they reaped in me. Truthfully, I was intellectually enjoying them more than they proved able to make me a clearer reflection of Christ. Though I had long considered sermons a useful tool in being a Christ-follower, I rarely considered how much they helped me become a more effective conduit of his love.

After leaving Fairview Church, I saw how good things such as sermons (in person and on-line), book studies, videos, and

Christian books could be bad when I found myself addicted to them. As a Christian who also consistently prayed and read the Bible, I would have argued that I was not dependent on them and could lay them aside. However, I would not relinquish them, even for a certain time, despite my conscience sometimes prompting me to feel that I should.

In the absence of a church home with its respective and prestigious pastor, God helped me to see the truth about my ways and my heart. First, I saw my stubbornness. Second, I saw how much I was emotionally attached to gifted orators. I came to acknowledge that sometimes I appreciated man's spoken words about God more than I esteemed God's spoken Word to me. Said another way, sometimes I enjoyed a pastor's delivery about a passage of scripture more than the scripture itself. I assumed that this phenomenon was not abnormal among Christians, so for a time, I did not experience sadness or conviction about it.

Removed from regular church services at any single congregation, I found that I was more honest with God and myself concerning my Christian practices. I was able to see my habits and preferences more clearly, causing me to feel grieved about gravitating to the words of man over those of God. I recognized that for several years, I was much more inclined to invest time reading Christian literature than the Bible itself, largely because I found books about Christian living to be more relatable and easier to understand. I simply justified that Christian literature and on-line sermons were supplemental, since I most commonly reached for them in the afternoon or evenings, while I generally read the Bible in the mornings.

Recognizing my impure and unholy affection toward God's living Word led me to change. I felt compelled to stop watching on-line sermons and ceased reading Christian literature apart from the Bible for an indefinite period of time. Doing so helped me to better esteem the Bible, relying foremost on God's Word rather than man's words about it. Even after I felt the freedom to listen to recorded sermons again, I found the appeal had largely waned. As a result, I also became more mindful and selective during the infrequent times I sought to listen to them. Additionally, when I started reading Christian literature again, I became cognizant about reading it disproportionately to the Bible. I came to respect the holy scriptures increasingly, accepting the fact that I may never understand portions of it as well as many pastors. But more than before, I have learned to value the room I have to wrestle with God through his Word, even without another man to help me in the ring.

Chapter 18

AUTHORITY

Be still, and know that I am God;
I will be exalted among the nations,
I will be exalted in the earth!
The Lord of hosts is with us;
The God of Jacob is our refuge. Selah

Psalm 46:10-11 (NKJV)

I am leery of man-made structures within God's church.

Upon my exit from Fairview Church, a few leaders approached me and asked what specifically I disagreed with concerning the proposal that the church had voted to pass. At the time, I found the question to be an odd one. I had not based my decision to leave on any one detail within the proposal but on the proposal itself. The elders' recommendation was not broken into parts; the congregation could vote to pass the proposal as a whole or not. I simply believed that God did not affirm what had been suggested by the church leaders and that he did not want his people to ratify it.

Since that time, I have more greatly considered a church's responsibility when facing a hard issue and the approach a congregation adopts to resolve it. While it was not the reason for my leaving, I have also thought about the structure of local church bodies, especially how they help or hinder congregations to solve problems facing them. Since leaving Fairview Church, my values have changed as far as what I would personally accept structure-wise within a local church body; particularly, I hold greater interest in knowing whether or not a church's structure welcomes the participation of all parishioners in problem solving or if it primarily empowers a select few.

At the time Fairview Church faced issues with capacity, the church body was not summoned and presented the problem. Members were not asked to pray about the issue as it manifested over time. Neither were they invited to share ideas or personal discernment regarding God's potential solution. At Fairview Church, the structure of the church and the responsibility that the leadership bore through that structure was what ultimately led to the proposal itself.

The proposal offered one solution to the issue of capacity. Ultimately, the leaders of the church assessed an issue concerning the body, apart from the body. After gathering privately, they presented the problem and their proposed solution to the church. To the best of my recollection, only after presenting the proposal did they publicly and readily invite the congregation to go forth and pray.

In being asked to pray at that time, Fairview's congregants were essentially invited to intercede about the wisdom that leadership had sought, presumably received, and believed the body should employ. Looking back, I see the approach as having been largely backwards, including the order of involvement of the body; however, the scenario was not unruly or unreasonable based on the church's bylaws.

As a result of my experience, I would now strongly question taking part of a local church body if it maintained a structure that threatened to impede a church family from acting as one. I would not likely adhere to a local church body if its governing ways could prevent or undermine God's body from solving a problem together, from start to finish, particularly one impacting the entire congregation. In my situation, the parishioners of Fairview were presented a solution that was offered by the leadership, but the cost associated with the solution would directly and indefinitely impact current attendees and future congregants (quite possibly, without the latter group of people knowing).

Prior to the vote surrounding the new broadcast location, the structure within Fairview had been of little concern to me. But when the vote transpired, the church's structure became hugely consequential in my life because I was required to "actively" submit to its design. At the time the vote took place, I could do nothing to circumvent the church's structure or alter how it impacted the scenario before me. I was one of thousands who were suddenly "bound" by Fairview's bylaws. As a result, regardless if congregants acknowledged it or felt favorably about it, each one had to accept being given a solution instead of an invitation to seek God's remedy—together and from the start. Having faced the situation, and believing our course of action did not honor God's design of his local church, I now look at church structures and their governments with increased scrutiny and skepticism.

Having Fairview's elders present their solution to the congregation was not an authentic representation of God's body seeking his wisdom together. Though leaders can benefit a church body, assuming they serve the body while protecting the members' best interest, esteeming and trusting them never abdicates the responsibility of the rest of the body to pray and seek God's wisdom together. Moreover, it is unhealthy for congregants to rely on specific people to discern God's direction, and the humblest of individuals would not want a church body to do this, even if congregants were obliged or so inclined.

Church structures or governments limit God when they lead members of a church to problem solve by looking to pastors instead of God; meanwhile, reverence for God becomes undermined by the church body's respect for its leaders. As demonstrated through the elders' proposal at Fairview, looking to leaders can cheat God of the opportunity to work through others while robbing all parishioners of the chance to be answerable to his request.

In any decision facing a church, seeking God's direction and wisdom is the only noble thing to do. But how can a local church discern God's best while failing to honor his design of the body? That design includes a divine orchestration of many members, all learning to work together while seeking solutions for the common good. Otherwise, church members can fall prey to becoming apathetic within Christ's body, even unknowingly, since the fruit coming from it is largely inconspicuous. For instance, dependency upon leaders which is dangerous can appear to be honoring authority which is respectworthy.

Moreover, man-made and subjective church structures can ultimately work against pastors instead of aiding their success. For instance, I have always assumed that most pastors lead church members with the hope of seeing them mature in their faith. However, a church that maintains a structure which prevents a pastor from involving congregants in difficult matters ultimately works to stunt the growth of parishioners. As a result, a pastor may lead with the intent to see congregants mature, but the church's structure may actually undermine that objective. Therefore, when leaders do not involve fellow congregants in problem solving, whether the respective church structure permits their involvement or not, leaders ultimately foster a spirit of dependency, not maturity, in those they shepherd.

Church members then learn to trust church leaders to solve congregational issues and are content to let them, a behavior that I believe I witnessed at Fairview. The result is not just sad but dangerous. Congregants grow accustomed to following a select few, inadvertently learning that they should not expect to engage God collectively, even about issues the church body encounters as a whole. As a result, parishioners come to instinctively put their faith in the Christians whom they trust and admire most, placing greater confidence in the ability of others to follow God than their own ability to do the same.

When I was a part of Fairview Church, I subconsciously suspended a lot of personal responsibility each week as I took my seat in the sanctuary. I maintained a sense of trust in the leadership, and honestly, the byproduct of that trust was a feeling of great comfort. Throughout the week in my personal life, I was at risk of facing numerous hard situations. Frankly, I had no desire to walk into church and potentially encounter another. In large part, the church represented a refuge from problems in my life, not a setting in which I cared to be subjected to more.

Weekend church services felt like an escape, a safe place. I had an inherent sense of peace as a parishioner, knowing I had chosen my church home with assurance, partially because I felt confident in its leadership. Only when I was faced with a church-wide vote and took the time to look at the proposal created by Fairview's leadership did I question the fact that in every instance as a member and employee, I had given Fairview's leadership my trust, including the benefit of the doubt.

Being presented with a proposal that I discerned as contrary to the heart of God led me to clearly see the measure of faith that I had historically placed in my church leaders. Granting them my trust felt natural, but I realized that doing so was not necessarily prudent. Questioning my tendency to follow church leaders felt foreign and counter-intuitive. However, upon leaving Fairview Church, I better grasped the responsibility that I assumed in extending my trust to another. For the first time, I saw that my "blanket trust" in a church's leadership could be a disservice to Christ's body while also undermining my own walk with God.

I sometimes wonder what might have happened if Fairview's leaders had approached the greater church body and simply expressed their questions and concerns over the existing seating capacity. I can only imagine what might have transpired had they invited the body into the process of seeking God's perspective. Given the opportunity, I also wonder how God may have worked through various congregants to alleviate the concern. While I don't know what would have happened, I heartily question that God would have directed the entire body to a solution tied predominantly to a bank.

I believe the experience that I had at Fairview Church was a first-hand lesson about how easily men choose their own prescription over God's power and how quickly people prioritize having answers in-hand over waiting on the Lord's timing and directives. Through it, I am convinced that men's remedies, mistaken as the Lord's, lead local church bodies to cheap but expensive versions of what God might otherwise do. Meanwhile, I believe God is robbed of glory as short-sighted solutions are ascribed to him, as if he was the one to suggest them.

Despite the sins and failings of man, I know God is able to use all things. I do not doubt God's ability to work through the church that I left, one I continue to pray for. Leaving my job and church came at a cost, but the transaction left me standing with an overall yield I never imagined. Through my experiences at Fairview and my decision to leave the church, I gained what has been invaluable: an opportunity to know and trust God more and the wherewithal to share about it with others.

Fairview Church and its Loan:

The proposed years to pay off the debt and the interest rate of the loan were not presented to the congregation at the time of the vote, at least not that I was aware. After the congregation affirmed the proposed recommendation, if leaders disclosed the terms of the loan to the parishioners at the time the loan closed, they did so after I had left Fairview.

For basic consideration, I have included a table of various loan terms. The amounts shown below were determined using a basic on-line mortgage calculator and assume the total borrowed is $39.9 million dollars:

Total Years to Pay Off Loan	% Rate	Total Paid	Total Interest Paid	Interest Paid Per Month (Averaged)
10	4%	$48,476,172.00	$8,576,172.00	$71,468.10
10	5%	$50,784,169.00	$10,884,169.00	$90,701.41
10	6%	$53,156,616.00	$13,256,616.00	$110,417.80
15	4%	$53,124,387.00	$13,224,387.00	$73,468.82
15	5%	$56,794,798.00	$16,894,798.00	$93,859.99
15	6%	$60,605,797.00	$20,705,797.00	$115,032.21
20	4%	$58,028,676.00	$18,128,676.00	$75,536.15
20	5%	$63,197,362.00	$23,297,362.00	$97,072.34
20	6%	$68,605,438.00	$28,705,438.00	$119,605.90
25	4%	$63,182,070.00	$23,282,070.00	$77,606.90
25	5%	$69,975,428.00	$30,075,428.00	$100,251.43
25	6%	$77,122,878.00	$37,222,878.00	$124,076.26

EPILOGUE

After submitting my resignation, I worked a few additional months at Fairview Church and gradually tapered my hours. I left the office for the last time on a cold, winter day in the middle of January. A few months later, I received a text from a dear friend, Victoria, who lives just south of New Haven. She was texting me from a marriage retreat a few hours away, one orchestrated by her church.

Victoria had just met a new acquaintance, Emily White, a warm and disarming young woman who was somewhat new to the congregation. The retreat spanned the weekend, and afforded Victoria and Emily the chance to get to know one another.

Victoria's text explained how Emily had previously attended Fairview Church and worked there full-time, just as I had. Emily had developed concerns about the church, enough that she eventually left. Realizing our stories were similar, Victoria felt inclined to tell me about Emily, suspecting she and I might like to meet.

As Victoria texted me about her new friend, I was surprised that I had never heard Emily's name previously, either as a fellow Fairview member or former staff worker. I was also taken aback to learn how much her situation paralleled mine. I gladly took Emily's contact information and suspected we might meet one day.

That day came about a year later. At that time, my manuscript was several months underway, though largely laying dormant. I decided to reach out to Emily upon finding myself feeling a bit alone, still bearing a heavy heart about Fairview Church as I continued to process some of my observations from the years that I had been a part of it.

Emily and I met at a coffee shop, and with our guards instinctively down, we quickly connected with ease and honesty. She shared her story which sounded much like my own. She and her family were highly invested at Fairview Church, and she had been pleased to accept a position among its staff. As in my case,

Emily soon felt uneasy due to certain things she witnessed, but when she shared her concerns with her husband, he instinctively encouraged her to resume a positive attitude and to dispel notions that might appear nitpicky or critical.

However, in the months that followed, Emily and her husband both developed doubts about the church, and their family decided to leave. Prior to their exit, she and her husband sought a meeting with the lead pastor, but as in my case, he listened to their perspectives without ultimately sharing their concerns.

As I listened to Emily's account, I felt moved by her experience, humbled that she had happily joined the staff and sadly forsaken it, approximately 18-months before I was ever hired. Emily and I sat together emptying our hearts, sharing concerns about Fairview, observations that had remained in our minds even after being apart from the church for some time.

Eventually, I leaned over and asked Emily a question, one I sometimes found myself pondering:

Does any responsibility remain outstanding?

I knew she and I had done our due diligence in deciding to leave, but I wondered if our overall experience was relevant to a broader sphere of people in a way that it warranted being shared.

Upon ruminating aloud and at a high level, we agreed that every Christian must demonstrate wisdom and discernment concerning the congregation they choose to attend. We also acknowledged that people ultimately see what they want to see, as human nature leads our hearts to feel favorably toward things we love; meanwhile, our line of sight often tends to follow.

Emily and I also concurred that, in our opinion, congregants of Fairview Church were suffering from a certain blindness. We believed those affected included staff members whose livelihood appeared to depend on the church's well-being, almost as if they were inoculated from seeing Fairview's state as anything other than healthy. But apart from staff members, we believed all congregants were able to see reasons for concern, even in the present, if their minds and spirits were better attuned.

I agreed with Emily that every parishioner maintained a

duty to be a responsible one, but I also shared with her how I felt the congregants at Fairview were becoming increasingly desensitized about the church, even while continuing their affiliation with it. I confessed that if I had never been a staff member at the church, I suspected I would be among the first to overlook any supposed signs of illness within it.

In considering such a scenario, I told her that I would likely be upset if I never knew that someone among the staff had concerns over the congregation, long before I recognized such issues with my own eyes, so much that they chose to leave the church and their paid position there.

As I spoke honestly with Emily, I realized I had answered my own question. Without a doubt, I felt compelled to share my story. Though uncomfortable, I knew I needed to include certain details, not limited to a few that led me to leave Fairview. Among them were personal sins God revealed to me, things I saw only after my resignation.

I confided in Emily about the manuscript I had begun, a certain work I was ill-prepared to polish and that no literary agent whom I had queried showed interest in representing. Unmoved by the mountain I described, Emily encouraged me in my endeavor.

From that morning forward, she and I continued to intercede for the culmination of this book and each set of hands that now hold it.

FINAL THOUGHTS FROM THE AUTHOR

Every person has a story; I just chose to put mine on paper. The decision was a stretch for me since my definition of risk is trying a new flavor of ice cream. Truth be told, I valued the vision to complete this book more than I esteemed my ability to actually do it. At the same time, I feared not finishing what I had started or not finishing in a worthy manner. Having completed this feat to the best of my ability, I invite readers to embark on their own God-inspired endeavors.

FIND STORIES THAT INSPIRE THE HEART

For me, a few have been:

The life story of Katie Davis, captured in her book: *Kisses from Katie*

The story of Gret Glyer and his creation of *DonorSee*, reflected in his book: *If the Poor Were Next Door*
(a project launched through *Kickstarter*)

The life story of Jeremy Cowart, told in his own words on YouTube: *I'm Possible – Photographer Jeremy Cowart*

The story of Trent Taylor's childhood, told in his book: *Shattered No More*

The story of Cassie Bernell and her family, reflected in the book: *She Said Yes*

The story of *Underground People* captured by P.J. Accetturo (Vimeo) (a project launched through Kickstarter)

The book *Transformation* by Matt Bird

DAYDREAM, PRAY, LISTEN, ACT:

These might help:

Restless, a book by Jennie Allen

The Power of Vulnerability, a TED Talk by Brene Brown

The Power of Introverts, a TED Talk by Susan Cain

(By the way, I don't know any of these people, and they don't know me.)

www.ingramcontent.com/pod-product-compliance
Lightning Source LLC
Chambersburg PA
CBHW031117080526
44587CB00011B/1016